IN DEFENCE OF LITERATURE

FOR

john calder

FIFTY YEARS OF PUBLISHING LITERATURE, POLITICS AND THE ARTS

IN DEFENCE OF LITERATURE

FOR

john calder

BY HIS FRIENDS AND ADMIRERS

FIFTY YEARS OF PUBLISHING LITERATURE, POLITICS AND THE ARTS

Mosaic Press

TORONTO PARIS NEW YORK

Canadian Cataloguing in Publication Data

Main entry under title:

In defense of literature: John Calder: fifty years of publishing literature,
   politics and the arts

Includes bibliographical references.
ISBN 0-88962-625-1

1. Calder, John. 2. Publishers and publishing — England — Biography.
3. Catalogs, Publishers' — England. I. Aster, Howard. II. Land, Amy, 1974-

Z325.C2512 1998   070.5'092   C98-932818-X

Published by MOSAIC PRESS, P.O. Box 1032, Oakville, Ontario, L6J 5E9,
Canada. Offices and warehouse at 1252 Speers Road, Units #1&2, Oakville,
Ontario, L6L 5N9, Canada and Mosaic Press, 85 River Rock Drive, Suite 202,
Buffalo, N.Y., 14207, USA.

Mosaic Press acknowledges the assistance of the Canada Council and the
Dept. of Canadian Heritage, Government of Canada, for their support of our
publishing programme.

THE CANADA COUNCIL | LE CONSEIL DES ARTS
FOR THE ARTS | DU CANADA
SINCE 1957 | DEPUIS 1957

Printed and bound in Canada

MOSAIC PRESS, in Canada:
1252 Speers Road, Units #1&2,
Oakville, Ontario, L6L 5N9
Phone / Fax: (905) 825-2130
E-mail:
cp507@freenet.toronto.on.ca

MOSAIC PRESS, in the USA:
85 River Rock Drive, Suite 202,
Buffalo, N.Y., 14207
Phone / Fax: 1-800-387-8992
E-mail:
cp507@freenet.toronto.on.ca

acknowledgments

Acknowlegments

Every publisher owes his existence first and foremost to authors, then to booksellers and then to readers. On behalf of all those associated with this Festschrift, we would like to thank all John Calder's authors, all the booksellers who have supported John and all the millions of readers who have read books published by John Calder.

Many thanks to all the contributors to this volume for the gracious essays, anecdotes and thoughts. Thank you to Jim Haynes and David Applefield who encouraged, pushed, cajoled and provided the energy for the completion of this volume. A special 'thank you' to Amy Land whose devotion to the project was unfailing, at all times. She compiled the text, including the labourious task of the bibliography, and she applied her considerable design talents to make this book possible. André Derval and Olivier Corpet of IMEC, l'Institut Mémoires de l'édition contemporaine, have provided the archival base for John Calder's considerable collection of papers and documents.

John Calder has many, many, many friends, admirers, colleagues and supporters in many countries. To all of them, now and over five decades of publishing, thank you.

table of contents

Section Four

Books Published by John Calder

"For John Calder with failing words my unfailing affection, appreciation of his efforts on behalf of my work, admiration of his resistance to the slings and arrows."

Sam Beckett
1. 10. 89

Card from Samuel Beckett, written shortly before the playwright's death, paying tribute to John Calder

preface

Howard Aster

*F*ifty years in publishing... one-half of a century....five decades....It is a very long time.

Not just to have survived, but to have sustained a publishing house during a period when independent publishers have disappeared at an alarming rate. Today, corporatisation has displaced the judgement of publishers by the edict of accountants and actuaries and the elusive logic of 'market forces' seems to have crippled the pursuit of literary excellence.

John Calder is, indeed, a survivor! He may well be what the British newspaper *The Independent* called him – "The last of the gentleman publishers." Independence is important to John Calder because it preserves the ability of anybody - in this case the Publisher - to exercise judgement about what books should be published or not without interference from others. It is the work itself which must be judged or deemed publishable - worthy of becoming a public document. For a publisher, this is fundamentally both an act of courage and a risk. But most of all it must be an ethical act. It is his or her statement that 'I deem this work worthy of becoming part of a literary or intellectual or cultural tradition to which I, as publisher, in my own small way, contribute as well.' It is an act of responsibility, an ethical act, not an anonymous statement by the market place, or the actuarial judgement of the 'bottom line'.

So why a Festschrift?

In this age of extreme commercialism, celebrations have become warped. It is success defined in market terms that is noted and celebrated. This Festschrift for John Calder is a way of noting and, yes, celebrating 50 years of the existence and value of an individual, important publisher. It is a way of celebrating the books John Calder has published, celebrating the astonishing array of authors that John Calder has published, and celebrating the man himself!

John Calder is a very modest man. When I first suggested to him that some others and I wanted to organise a Festschrift for him, he stated categorically that ' it was a bad idea. There was no need...it would be better to devote your time to other matters.' He tried to dissuade us from this 'act of folly.' However, John Calder's friends, colleagues and associates clearly disagreed.

But there is another reason for this Festschrift. John himself organised and published two Festschrifts - *Beckett at Sixty* (1967) and *as no other dare fail* (1986). The latter book is subtitled, For Samuel Beckett on his 80th Birthday by his friends and admirers.

Let me quote from John's own introduction to *Beckett at Sixty*:

"And therefore this book. It is not put together for the benefit of its subject who will chuck it away in disgust and who is no more interested in being sixty than he was interested in being one. It is not published for the benefit of the publisher who will do as well out of it as the publisher of the narrator of "From An Abandoned Work." It is written for the benefit of the contributors, who would honestly prefer the author not read what they have said, but who want to say basically that they love him, or admire him, or that they are grateful to him, for making it possible to be grateful for something in our unspeakable century, by simply creating a little body of print that no man can read from beginning to end and still say, 'I am the same person. I am unchanged.'"

What John Calder wrote about Samuel Beckett in 1967 is surely applicable to him today.

Thank you, John, for having the courage, foresight and insight to have created a large body of printed words, a veritable library of many of the most important literary works to have been published in the second half of the twentieth century. Nobody who will read the books you have published could possibly say that "I am the same person today as I was before I read the Calder publications."

A genuine publisher is above all else an ethicist, a person who exercises ethical judgements all the time. He or she is given the unenviable task of saying publicly, "I believe this work is better than that work." And, this judgement is based upon a set of moral standards which are open, public and, of course, as all human judgements are, they are debatable.

Let me offer yet another reason for "Why this Festschrift?" and, again, let me quote John, this time from his essay entitled "Embarrassing Mr. Beckett" published in *as no other dare fail.*

"A Festschrift such as this is first of all an opportunity for those who owe him so much to say 'thank you' to Samuel Beckett, not only for the supreme pleasure we have derived from the texts and the insight he has given us into the grim realities of the 'muck heap' we inhabit, but also for formulating, poetically and practically, an ethic by which to live.

"Samuel Beckett, that most modest of sages, does not welcome books such as this, and I hope it will not give him, embarrassment, but even if it does, it may, directly through its pin-pointing of the relevance of his writing to getting through life, and indirectly through guiding more readers to the most exciting and potent literary adventure of our time, prove of great value to those who face anguish, disappointment or tragedy, as we all must. It is a tribute, not so much to an anniversary, as to a realism that has had the courage to face the naked truth on a poisoned planet which is increasingly living on lies and pretence and where the tears of the world do not diminish. *Morituri te salutant!* We have been fortunate in such a time to have such a poet among us."

There are many mysteries to every human being and, of course, there are many mysteries to John Calder. But there are also a number of facts which are blatantly obvious.

John Calder chose to be a publisher. In his early twenties, he defied family, tradition and many other things to become a publisher. For John it was a wilful and very meaningful act – simultaneously an act of defiance, an act of definition and a moral act. I think that publishing for John today is no different. Circumstances may have changed, the pizzazz and the players may be different, but the act of publishing remains the same.

But what to publish? Again, there is no mystery here for John Calder.

John's studies and training in political economy and history revealed to him that the twentieth century is the cruellest of all centuries. Literature and the arts are the most vital of all the dykes that humanity has built for itself to withhold and withstand the onslaught of barbarism. The efforts to comprehend and withstand the endless ravaging of barbarism against civilisation is best understood and appreciated in literature and the arts. Hence, to publish literature and books on the arts is a further contribution to humanities efforts to withstand the seemingly endless onslaughts of barbarism.

There is another point of absolute clarity in the decisions as to what John has chosen to publish. From the moment that John determined that his fate was to publish books, he had a very clear and uncompromising vision. His family background and his education rooted him in three places simultaneously - Britain, North America and Europe. John has systematically tried to re-attach or reconnect the cultural currents of these three geographic regions. And, probably more than any other publisher, John has sought out writers and authors, translated them and tried to enrich the English language by publishing them for the English speaking world. He has been a one-man cultural agency, talent scout and literary impresario for the English language world.

John Calder has also sought to expand the boundaries of legitimate discourse in literature and the arts. Freedom is an extremely important value for John. Without freedom, the arts cannot flourish. There is a constant struggle which all publishers face - whether to test and expand the boundaries of public discourse in the arts, literature and politics, or to act within the constraints of accepted legitimacy. John has always tested and expanded the boundaries, often at great cost, but he has been consistently driven by defiance and principle.

For civilisation and culture to survive, perhaps, even flourish, the arts must never be tamed. The pressures to tame the arts are myriad - from religion to the boardrooms, from the market place to the politicians - everywhere there are enormous pressures to bridle and restrict the freedom of the arts. The career of John Calder, as an individual and as a publisher has been marked by his absolute devotion to unfetter the arts from any constraint.

John Calder has always acted to untame the arts, to let them defy the accepted standards, to challenge constantly complacency and passive acceptability. The books John has published in 50 years have all contributed to this principle of the untaming of the arts.

I well remember first meeting John Calder. I was struck by the fact that he was an immensely shy man. I still think so. His shyness tends to reinforce his immense sense of privacy on some matters. But there is also a powerfully paradoxical quality to John. He is astonishingly generous - intellectually, emotionally, financially, culturally. He has an openness about him which is increasingly rare among people. Many, many people have benefited from this generosity of spirit. John is both a natural iconoclast - although he is costumed, usually, in a three-piece suit - and a natural teacher.

All who have contributed to this book respect, admire and love John. Each of us, in our own way, has been touched and enriched by knowing this man and knowing how much he has enriched the literature of the English language.

What a better world it is now that John has published for 50 continuous years. Let us hope that the principles that have provoked his actions and the literary judgements that he has made can be 'cloned' to future generations.

Thank you, John!

Paris, September 1998

section one

section one

I

John Calder

1958

BOOKS

The Three-Headed Hydra

by John Calder

Janet Flanner, the American journalist who for many years, from the thirties onward, covered literary and expatriate Paris for American magazines, wrote in her introduction to one of the most important literary histories of the pre-war period:

In the evolution of literature the book publisher had-undeniably been the second main essential. Yet individually he had been rarely famed as the necessary major element connected with the appearance of a new great book, nor even much thanked by his reader. He has been literature's common carrier, like a donkey, with the authors and occasionally their weight of genius loaded on his back. (Hugh Ford, *Published in Paris*, 1975).

She was thinking of Sylvia Beach and of those other literary publishers whose names have been linked with a writer or a few writers to whom they gave attention and devotion well beyond the usual professional relationship, based on a mutual interest in making money from books. In thinking of the Hydra, the many-headed monster, whose heads were chopped off by Hercules only to have them grow back again. I see an analogy of that literature which rises time and again through, and in spite of, opposition, disapproval, censorship, fundamentalist ideology and the incomprehension of the plain reader (the last sentence of the "Proclamation" issued by the writers associated with *transition*, the most important of the English-language pre-war Parisian magazines, ended: "the plain reader be damned.").

It is the writing, damned or at first dismissed, that usually emerges as the significant literature of its time, and like the Hydra can be defined as "a thing hard to extirpate." Such literature may be cut back at first, but it will be kept alive by its devotees, often by other writers and friends, as happened with the Joyces and Kafkas of their day, until the academics and pundits are able to declare the writer a genius and his works as classics. Personally I see the Hydra as having three heads, the writer, the publisher and the bookseller. But others can be imagined, such as the literary agent, the librarian, the teacher, the proselytizing admirer. But only a few of the potential geniuses ever emerge into the light of day. I have seen enough real talent in manuscript to know that there are probably as many genuinely original unpublished writers as there are flowers blooming unseen in Gray's country churchyard, but there are never enough publishers willing or able to lose money on them: only a few are lucky. It is the publisher who takes the prime risk on a new author, and often he does not stay in business very long, but credit must also go to the genuine booksellers of taste (Sylvia Beach was both) who read a writer, recommend and sell him, sometimes having to face prosecution for the privilege of doing so.

The role of the bookseller as a purveyor of culture is often underestimated in literary history. Long before public libraries of any kind existed, booksellers not only sold books but produced them, often by subscription from their customers. For the two centuries before the twentieth, and more recently on a more specialized level – because so many books are published, and very few could be called in any way literary – the role of the bookseller in recognizing unusual talent, in helping it, either through publication or more commonly in stocking and promoting an author where others would not, has been crucial. A town with a good bookseller will often produce young people with intellectual curiosity and interests, whose minds he helps, often unwittingly, to develop and only the exceptional school-teacher is as important in this respect as the exceptional bookseller: if he is dedicated to his trade he becomes a centre of culture, and lucky is the small town or even village that has such an establishment. It is usually, although not necessarily, small and dusty with some new books and many old ones, where it is the author on the shelf that counts, not the edition or even necessarily its condition, although the true book-lover does enjoy handling a well-made book with good type, paper that will last, and a handsome binding. Sylvia Beach's Shakespeare and Company in Paris and Frances Stelloff's Gotham Book Mart in

New York were two of the most famous of such individualist book-shops that have become part of literary history, but they had their counterparts in London, Chicago, Berlin, Prague, Stockholm, and Milan before the watershed of Hitler, the greatest destroyer of culture in centuries, brought the arts in Europe to a temporary stop. The good bookseller does not just supply his customers, he also leads them.

If the exceptional bookseller is the tertiary member of a literary partnership, then what can be said of the publisher? I, the author, am one myself, and I have followed in the tradition of those who have given their names to their imprint, have published for interest and pleasure rather than profit, and have resisted the temptation to sell out for a pile of money at times when such offers were available. My career has been a curved arc that started in the early fifties, reached its highest point in the sixties, and then began a slow descent into the nineties. I have been a player in the literature of the postwar period and my literary success, as well as my lack of business sense, can be judged by my having published more Nobel Prize winners than any other publisher in Britain during that time, while making no money doing it, but this means little to the public: historically, the publisher is almost anonymous, less known to those who buy books than the bookseller who meets such readers, and is consequently recommended by one customer to another. Only a few publishers have had their names linked to an author, and even then usually only for his early years, such as Kurt Wolff to Kafka, and Fasquelle to Proust. The identification of Sylvia Beach with Joyce lies in her unique reputation as a bookseller who became an amateur publisher, a person who met writers, encouraged, admired and flattered them, and thereby became a "celebrity" as far as the public was concerned. My own identification, and it will not last too long, has been with Samuel Beckett, in my view one of the four great writers of the twentieth century, along with the previously mentioned Proust, Kafka and Joyce: to a lesser extent I am known for presenting in English the work of the "absurdist" playwrights and the school of fiction known as the *nouveau roman*.

Coming on my father's side from a line of Scottish crofters, who in the nineteenth century became successful brewers and whisky distillers, and on my mother's from French-Canadian *habitants*, of whom my maternal grandfather ended as a banker, I had no formal background in any literary field and taught myself by reading. The only quality I inherited from my tough ancestors was a certain stubbornness. From the beginning I wanted to acquire the learning that none

JOHN MINIHAN

Calder & Burroughs

John Calder and William S. Burroughs

of them had the time or inclination to develop, and from childhood, I wanted to write, and to read endlessly, being frustrated, like Henry Miller in his youth, at the difficulty of getting books. But I never really had much personal ambition for fame as a against scope, wanting to get things done, and I have a natural reticence, which means that I have never objected to being Janet Flanner's "common carrier," a backroom person out of the limelight.

Mine has been a literary life, partly among the expatriates of Paris in the decades that followed those of Sylvia Beach, James Joyce, Ernest Hemmingway, Kay Boyle, Caresse and Harry Crosby, Eugene and Maria Jolas, Gertrude Stein and her circle, George Antheil and Paul Bowles (a composer before he was a writer), Man Ray and the surrealists, Bryher and Robert McAlmon, Scott Fitzgerald, T.S. Eliot, Ezra Pound, Ford Maddox Ford and all the other names we associate with the twenties and thirties: some of them, like Henry Miller, bridge the pre-war and post-war worlds. The connection between what one does in life and the way in which one lives is the principal justification for biography and literary history: it is difficult, if not impossible, for a public figure, even a writer, to keep many secrets from biographers and the interested readers of the future; he is perhaps wise not to hide too much or he will be misunderstood, misinterpreted and have many fallacies tied to his name by future generations. Biographers have to imagine or invent their "facts" to fill the holes. Even the most reclusive of writers cannot afford to be too secretive.

Paris of the fifties and sixties has attracted nostalgia and interest in a later age of scarcity and decline. It was a time of growth and excitement lived under the threat of nuclear war, that encouraged those who were young to live intensely and fast, because extinction, even the end of the world, seemed always near. That age of positive thinking under threat later turned into a general pessimism about what was to come, which from the perspective of the nineties holds an infinite number of unknown futures. As the century draws to a close, we are all more cynical, aware of the presence of conspiracy, much of it criminal, in the shaping of present and future events, which was not a part of the awareness of earlier generations. We have come to take corruption and criminality for granted. No one is above suspicion any more, or is believed to represent what they pretend; there is not much surprise when an apparently clean tycoon or politician is unmasked. Electors vote for what they perceive as the lesser evil, not for what they really want, because no one will offer them that. Democracy has become a sham in every country where there are too many conflicting interests or ethnic minorities in collision. The re-emergence of tribalism in every society makes a mockery of democracy, which depends, for its existence and proper working on a knowledgeable, educated, aware and politically active electorate being given clear choices. Choices today are never clear, and this has led to an estrangement of the intellectual community, those who live by their talents as artists, teachers or media people, from the general population of those who simply want a good life, permanent employment and peace. Control still lies with an oligarchy which, although insecure, is indifferent to the well being of the majority. In the troubled times to come the arts will always continue to exist, because the artist will always find a way to express himself, even if he has no audience, but culture – the shared climate of imaginative and thought provoking activity that can only exist where life is otherwise apparently secure – is in ever-greater danger. Few politicians give culture more than lip service and in the United States it is usually too dangerous even to mention. George Bush, when he was president, could not admit to a liking for classical music, while in France, any politician who did not have at least a veneer of culture could never be elected. The French want to be led by those with good minds and good educations, Americans too often by the lowest common denominator, those who affect to be most like themselves. Although the arrival of much younger politicians like Bill Clinton and Al Gore had led one to hope that perhaps this might change. Alas, not! The British vote to support whatever will most hurt the class image of the class they hate most. There are different cultures in Britain and they tend to clash, cancelling each other out. The British seem to like living with dissatisfaction.

The relationship between art and culture is often confused. One can exist without the other. Culture is a climate in which one lives; it includes our working as well as our leisure lives, our attitudes, prejudices, pleasures and obligations; the arts are a part of it, but usually in so far as they are accepted, and have become anodyne and generalized, appealing almost invisibly, like *muzak*. Minority cultures often invade the larger ones because they are "discovered" and can enrich an art scene that has faded, whereas a culture seen as too foreign, irrelevant or imperialistic can be totally rejected by a community, country or a continent. Beethoven and Shakespeare have no place in African culture, nor do most modern equivalents, but Peter Brook and

John Cage would not be so alien there. On the other hand, African art, and some writers like Wole Soyinka and Chinua Achebe, have marginally invaded western culture. A general culture, as distinct from a high culture, is what is accepted at a given time, but it disintegrates under great stress, usually brought about by war, famine, earthquake or economic collapse. Art on the other hand, a principle component of high culture, is constantly created, but may not survive even a minor upset because it is fragile by nature; both the artist and his art can disappear because of malice or accident. The wars of the sixteenth century in Italy saw the destruction of all but a handful of the works of Leonardo da Vinci, and many other masters of the high culture of the high renaissance. Much poetry was written in the trenches during the first world war, but only a handful of it has survived, poetry having been the natural means of expression for the young officer class of Britain at the time, and most of it died in battle. One can only speculate on the art destroyed by the Nazis who killed so many artists. But new art has always continued to be created, although only a small part becomes a part of a majority culture. What can be said is that there is a culture of philistinism that stifles creativity – not its creation as much as its reception – and a culture of art, that by definition is necessary to a good society, one in which it is pleasant and stimulating to live. Unfortunately, when such a good society exists, and it is usually the result of special circumstances like the aftermath of a war and much individual and group effort, it tends to be destabilized by undemocratic forces, by power-lust and cupidity. Those who live in fortunate times quickly become complacent and make too little effort to defend what they have come to take for granted. Individualist publishers are not necessarily literary, but it is the literary, and to a great extent the political publishers – often they are the same – who change the world a little. I have admired many before my own time, although some, like Victor Gollanez, the product of an earlier age and morality, disapproved of me; my publishing did not conform to the Fabian ethic he epoused. I am aware of myself as sometimes being a loose cannon, and have always been considered eccentric by colleagues. My campaigns against censorship, and the campaigns of others have sometimes had the effect of opening doors to the random exploitation of sex and the cheapening of it, which I regret; sex should always have a mystery and a sense of wonder and excitement, not possible in the plastic age of Madonna, but we still have not lost the censors; they have shifted their ground, always finding new ways to

DAVID APPLEFIELD

❝ My colleagues and I believed
passionately in justice, in achieving
a better society, a freer and
more stimulating life, and not
just for ourselves... **❞**

— *John Calder*

control how we think, what we do, what we buy, which way we vote. Sex has become matter of fact and freely discussed, which is healthy enough; what is not healthy is the way it is exploited for gain, for the most cynical of reasons. Maurice Girodias, Barney Rosset and I, mavericks of the fifties and sixties, and others who have followed us after 1970, liberated sex to remove guilt and make it natural and enjoyable as it has always been for an uninhibited minority, and we did so by allowing authors to describe it honestly and poetically, as well as erotically; what counted for us all was the adventure; the financial gain, where there was one, was a fortuitous by-product.

Adventure is what my own career has been about. The "Lost Generation" that preceded us was in part deadly serious (Sylvia Beach *et al.*), partly romantically mad (Harry Crosby) and partly opening the doors to eclectic experiment (Eugene Jolas). This refers to the pre-war Paris scene, although similar things were happening in Germany, Britain and elsewhere. What followed, after the years of war, was an age of enjoyment, one we are unlikely to see again, perhaps never, in a world of growing population and shrinking amenity, with general culture and education (in the best sense) declining as specialization makes it harder to find, among those under forty, individuals who are fully rounded, with a taste for knowledge outside their particular field of activity. My colleagues and I believed passionately in justice, in achieving a better society, a freer and more stimulating life, and not just for ourselves. All of us, in our individual and eccentric ways, made personal sacrifices to bring what we had in ourselves to others.

Most lives end in tragedy and every life ends somehow. We are often the authors of our own tragedies, led by a Will-o-the-wisp or a *Ferner Klang*, an evasive sound we feel compelled to follow, as in Shreker's too little-known expressionist opera. It sometimes seems to me that life is like a mist in which we wander, half lost, half thinking we know the path ahead, in a landscape where our lives cross and recross at random the lives of others, where ambitions become distorted, hopes blunted, and a malignant puppet-master pulls the strings. I have already mentioned Beckett as the writer with whom, as a publisher, I have been most associated. He has been much more than a friend and an author I helped to establish; I have found in his writing, which is still part of my everyday consciousness after the man and our friendship are gone, great comfort and ever-greater aesthetic enjoyment; Beckett's parables satisfactorily and convincingly describe our existence, which can never be objectively explained. In one of his

19

most powerful metaphorical novels *How It Is*, he sees all mankind crawling or swimming through a sea of mud, trying desperately to stay on the surface, while the pull drags us downward; some get a temporary relief as they crawl over others, or give some respite to others as they are pushed down by those who crawl over them. This grim parable offers no hope, but there is still comfort in recognizing our real world in it. Beckett's is cathartic art, depicting real horror, but he enables us to live with it because it is art on the highest poetic level; the excitement of his work enables the thinking individual to escape in his mind the daily torture of living and facing reality. That brings me to my other motivation as a publisher and an activist in the world of the arts, and occasionally of politics (I have stood for office, but being outspoken, have never been elected); I have tried to spread an awareness of the art that creates awareness, the presence of which, whether as creation or appreciation, separates mankind from the other species with which we share the planet, and without which, to quote Nietzsche, "Life is a desert."

*From **The Garden of Eros**, a tour of post World War II literary Paris and contemporary culture, from FRANK #16/17*

section two

section two

II

NEW BOOKS

Calder 1964

Life

Growing
Sowing
Mowing
Knowing
Going

- *John Calder*

An Interview

growing

I come from an upper middle class background. I have two grand-
fathers who were pretty successful in business. One of them inherited a brewery in Scotland from his father as well as the distillery that
made whisky. And also they had timber yards, they imported wood
from Scandinavia, from Canada, and they also had forests in Scotland.
And there was also a great deal of land in Scotland, approximately a
hundred thousand hectares. I also had a Canadian grandfather who
was a farm boy, who was successful and developed business interests
and started a bank in Montreal, and he was French-Canadian. But the
connection between the two families came through whiskey, because
during the American prohibition it was not allowed to make whisky,
beer or any alcohol in the United States so it was smuggled in from
Canada. From Scotland my family sent whisky to Canada and from
there it went to the United States. And at this time Joseph Kennedy
was the American ambassador in London and we know that he had
big interest in distilleries outside the United States and he was involved in smuggling, and that is why my family knew the Kennedys
when they were about twelve to eighteen years old.

My father was sent out by his uncle, his father's brother to Canada,
where he met my Canadian grandfather and that's when he married
my mother. And I was actually born in Canada, because my mother
would not trust doctors except in her own town, but I grew up in

DAVID APPLEFIELD

66 My grandfather said universities are very bad for young men, they would never be interested in real work. **99**

– John Calder

Scotland and in boarding schools in England. But always I was told I would be a brewer. And the brewery was in a very small little dull town in Scotland, where nothing ever happens. My grandfather said universities are very bad for young men, they would never be interested in real work. He meant that I would not want to go and live in a small town where there is no culture. But I went to university anyhow, because my mother could afford to send me there. My mother married again after the war, my father died in '44, and she married a man who wanted to run everybody's life and I was going to Oxford but he said no, it would be more interesting to go to Europe. And I said yes, please, I'll go to the Sorbonne. He said no, no I would do no work in Paris, better to go to a serious place like Zurich. So I went to Zürich to study National Okonomie to be a banker. I had no intention of being a banker, I mean I got my Doktorat in Zurich, but just. What I really studied were the things that interested me, which was literature and music and theatre and you know, culture generally. And there I fell in love with a Hollywood film actress who was in Zürich. I was preparing for my final exams, when I fell in love with her. And she was going to London, so I followed her to London and there I married her in 1949. And then I had seven years of great trouble because first of all she was very extravagant, second, I had a little bit of money that my father left me when he died, but nothing much else. While I started up writing for a newspaper, she was always in a film crowd and she made life very, very difficult for me and everybody wanted to go to bed with her all the time, so I was always fighting off competition, often very powerful people in the film industry. We finally broke the marriage up in 1957, at which point I became involved with an opera singer who was a Croat. We married in 1960 and that gave me many more troubles. So all the things going wrong in my life are my own fault for making two bad marriages. Two interesting women but, you know, when the passion wears off you find you have people who were very different from yourself and life is not so easy. Also I do not think that my character was made for marriage, you know, I'm not the sort of person that settles down. I went to work for my uncle in the beginning of 1950, and for seven years I worked for him in his timber business. I was very successful, very good at selling, so I made a lot of money on commission. And in 1949, I also started a little publishing company because at that point I was a poet. My poems were published in magazines, little magazines, everywhere and I had a little bit of a reputation and the favour of publishers who read my poems and said: "We would like these, we don't like those, if you'd write more like these we will publish a volume." But then I had a big fight with my wife, she destroyed my poetry, so I said: "Well, finished." Now my publishing company, although I was working at another business, was built up over the seven years till 1957. '57 I left the timber business, my uncle was very old, he had lost control, he was ninety five, out of the business, and I knew there was no future for me there, because there were a lot of jealousies with the other people around the company. I had become a director, but a director always pushed to the sidelines. I then gave all my energies to publishing. My great uncle died in 1962 and he left me his house in Scotland and his estate, and I turned it into a public theatre and gave a festival there: I did plays and operas and concerts, and for thirteen years we were very successful. And the reason it ended was because I was sabotaged by my second wife. Too long a story to tell here, but it caused me enormous financial problems. I had to sell the house; I had a divorce and law proceedings that are not yet finished. I've been more than two hundred days in court with her.

sowing

The first book I published came out in 1950. It was called *A Spy Has No Friends* and, I forget the name of the author, but it doesn't matter. In those days any book where you could find the paper sold very well. And then I began doing translations of books that I had read in other languages, books that didn't exist in English. I did quite a lot of Russian translations, Chekhov and Tolstoy. And then I began going to America to look for books. The McCarthy period was a time when quite well known American writers could not find a publisher anymore because they had been attacked as being left wing. So I was able to get a number of very good novelists, one was Albert Maltz, who was a big playwright in the 1930s. He had written many Hollywood films during the war that they discovered were favourable to Russia. I published his novels and he brought other authors to me. There was Martha Dodd, who was dismissed by the university because of her opinions and she was the daughter of an American ambassador who lost his job because his daughter was left wing. The novel was called *The Searching Light* and it was about the witch-hunt at American universities. I had a list of maybe thirty or forty books that came from America, that could not be published in the United

States. And I published one very important book about the Rosenberg case. Julius and Ester Rosenberg were accused of being atom spys and they were electrocuted. And that was a book about their trial that suggested that there were many irregularities. I imported part of the American edition to be bound up in Britain.

I was, in the early 1950s, very involved in political publishing, mainly because it was possible to get books from the United States in this climate. And then as a result of that I also began publishing books about political problems in Britain and Europe. In 1958, when de Gaulle came to power, many books came out about the behaviour of paratroops in Algeria. Most of the paratroops by the way were Germans and were ex-SS who had managed to escape because the foreign legion never asked any questions, they took in anybody. So I published a book called *La Question* in France and *The Question* in English. It was when they expected there would be a civil war in France. And that book sold out five thousand copies in two days, and I printed another ten thousand copies, which I sold in the next week. That was a big bestseller. And then I went on with a number of other books about colonial issues and I became very unpopular with the right wing in Britain, because I was publishing books exposing scandals and particularly the behaviour of British troops in colonial countries that were trying to get their freedom.

I remember I published *Der grune Heinrich* of Gottfried Keller. I did a lot of Goethe and I did a lot of Schiller and I did Storm and Eichendorff, many German classics, because nobody at that point was offering me contemporary literature. But then, on various trips to Paris, I began reading contemporary French books. And then I saw Beckett's *Waiting for Godot* when it first came out in London and I went to meet him.

But in the meantime my letter asking for the rights had gone to a wrong address and arrived one post behind that of Faber. And because that play was beginning to be a success in London, Faber bought it. So when I met Beckett it seemed he already had a publisher and that I would not be able to do anything. But then Faber turned down the novels, because they thought they were obscene. By that time I knew Beckett very well, and we had spent many nights out in Montparnasse talking, drinking, you know, we had many of the same interests. And then Beckett was the first author I bought from Editions de Minuit, but the books that he had written in English I bought directly from him. And also his poetry and, you know, everything else that he wrote, except for the plays. But there's one play I published because he wrote it and dedicated it to me, I think to make it possible that we had one play: *Come and go, Kommen und Gehen*.

I went to see Ionesco when he was still totally unknown, and said I would like to publish his plays that I had read or seen and he said, "Well, I don't have a French publisher yet, it's very difficult, you know." So I had to wait a year till Gallimard took him on and then I made a contract with Gallimard. I would go round the French publishers, I would get books and I would read them, and so I built up a very strong list of contemporary French fiction, a lot of the new theatre but also the nouveau roman. Simultaneously I was finding British writers, I was finding some American writers, I got Burroughs, I got Heinrich Boll, Reinhard Lettau, writers from almost everywhere.

From the late 50s throughout the 60s I began going every year to Frankfurt, where of course you make more contacts, and you come across more authors. The early 60s was the age when publishers who were enthusiastic about literature, who wanted to expand their list, would meet, would lunch, would have dinner together, would exchange information and it lead to a great deal of translation. That ended before 1970, when so many of these good authors didn't sell in translation. They might have a big reputation in their own country, but somehow it did not go over into the other language. On top of which, of course, I was competing with big publishers who were publishing much easier literature, and it got to a point where booksellers knew that my imprint meant highbrow, difficult, small sales. So even if I took on an author who would potentially be more popular, he would not sell well with me, whereas he would with somebody else, because they were afraid of the imprint. But, of course, I was popular with small, specialized booksellers that liked what I did, and who would give space to my books. So I had to build up a little network of bookshops not just in Britain but in Australia, in New Zealand and European bookshops who sold English books, that knew my books and respected them and were willing to stock them and buy them again when they sold and talk about them and so on. So the intellectual list gradually built up. But one reason why the more intellectual authors began to sell better was because in the early 60s I had an opportunity to publish a few authors who were certain to sell well if I was not prosecuted.

mowing

Our success during the 1960s came very largely out of the gradual acceptance of the new generation growing up that had been educated by the Labour government of more intellectual types of European literature. Publicity we received helped a great deal, for my other activities and also the fact that I suddenly had become a publisher of bestselling writers, Henry Miller and so on. I had a string of books for about two years, and they did very well. That continued until 1968 when I was prosecuted for *Last Exit to Brooklyn*, which was a prosecution that took two years and was very expensive and very dangerous. But I started an anti-censorship society that helped finance it and also financed other cases for other people after that.

At this time, of course, I was publishing a lot of theatre, many plays, I'd been publishing books on music which is one of my passions, and I had a lot of opera, and later on I started a series of opera guides that are maybe fifty per cent of our income today. During the 60s I was perhaps the most fashionable publisher, one of the most talked about.

The subsidies started in 1964 when the Labour government came to power and already in the 60s I would get the occasional subsidy for a very expensive translation of a book that was necessary but we obviously sold very slowly. They started putting in programmes making it possible for writers to receive some money for six months or a year to be able to write. And then big publishers were approached to take on some minority writers with subsidies. But then in the 1970s suddenly we were making losses every year and I inquired whether it might not be possible for us to get, instead of having to fill out form after form for each book, to maybe make an application for a whole year for a whole programme. We were finally told that they would give us a grant if we turned ourselves into a trust, a non-profit distributing company, and then we began getting subsidies that increased until the time Margaret Thatcher came in.

Now we had lost a great deal of money on the *Last Exit to Brooklyn* case, which we won after two years but again it was not a book that sold well. And then we had no more bestsellers after that and it was carrying on with solid literary titles that had a slow sale. People were reading less, the libraries were short of money and couldn't buy books, newspapers were being bought up by big proprietors who wanted to reduce the intellectual level of their readers. The whole Thatcher ethos was to downgrade education, take money away from the arts, away from the libraries and to stop subsidizing books that made people more intelligent; there was a general decline from the early 1970s onward. So one way or another we kept on going, kept on struggling. We lost many of our commercial authors, other ones, of course, would have nowhere to go if we weren't there anymore, nobody would publish them. And we had problems with our building in Soho which we rented, where we had been for thirty years. We couldn't pay royalties, we had big debts, couldn't print books, we went through a very bad time. Now we are in one little small room near King's Cross.

The other thing that happened in about 1970 is that the division of the market between British and American publishers stopped. Increasingly American publishers had London offices and they didn't want to sell rights. And then British publishers had to do the same the other way around. So we had a double market and you had to have offices in both places. And we lost money through booksellers going bankrupt and through distributors going bankrupt. And also I had to realize that my sales had dropped. The reason was that I had salesmen who were not interested in my books. They would carry fifty catalogues and mine was the last one that anybody looked at and then they would sell two books. But every time someone went into a bookshop to order one of my books, they got a commission on it. So in the end I said I would do all the selling myself. And that was the biggest overhead we had, the costs of salesmen. So I got rid of them and I do it all myself now. Two days a week I go and sell books. Fortunately I'm good at selling, and it's easy because I know the books.

knowing

Today we are facing doomsday. Unfortunately people do not think very far ahead. They do not realize the dangerous situation we are in. In the 1950s everybody was afraid of atomic war, maybe it could start by accident. It never happened but one lived in a feeling every day might be the last day of the world. I know that feeling very well. In 1958, I went to jail with Bertrand Russell protesting against the atom bomb. And I feel we're getting back to that today, I mean there is civil war everywhere, and nationalism is reemerging, I think fascism is coming back and just the last time I came I found in the doorway a propaganda leaflet from the National Front for the propa-

DAVID APPLEFIELD

❝ Increasingly, all American writers want to do is write to make money and be famous... **❞**

– *John Calder*

ganda on the unemployment beginning, we can see the collapse of capitalism coming, it must going to be another big depression. And the literary scene is unrecognizable. There had been various panels here at the book fair, but nobody is talking about the past; nobody is talking about today or tomorrow. Where are we going? What is this going to be, I mean obviously whatever today's literature is going to be it's going to return to a more committed kind of literature. But right now people are imitating old models all the time, trying to do what's been done. And increasingly particularly all American writers want to do is write to make money and be famous, but they are not particularly interested in the quality of what they are doing. People are only aware of crisis when it's on top of them. They cannot see ahead. So now we have the crisis of eating beef, but I've been seeing this coming for the last three years. The minute the government says something is safe, I know it's not safe. The air we breathe is getting more toxic the whole time. So I'm certain there'll be some nuclear disasters, this year, next year. Very soon, because there are so many dangerous reactors and they are not being properly looked after. And there are also a large number of weapons, terrible weapons, that are gradually going to get into the hands of terrorists. And there are certain forms of blackmail that cannot be resisted. If there is an atomic bomb underneath the city in which you live, you have to give them anything they ask for, you cannot refuse, otherwise the whole city blows up.

I think you have to do something similar to what happened in the early years of the century when expressionism boomed. It was a time when people met, talked, decided what they didn't like, began to talk about what should be done. What one has to do is see what is needed, not just for the world, but for the arts. There has to be a new direction. And it comes out of people meeting. When people who are intelligent meet and discuss things and they see a gap, they see where something is missing, and then they say: "How can I create that?" And one might do it in music and one might do it in the theatre and one might do it in poetry and another might do it in a novel and another might do it in painting. I mean opera started, because a group of amateurs who liked to play instruments decided that there was no current music that had any dramatic intensity and they wanted to recreate the Greek drama. So they invented this new art form. The expressionists, you know, said, "We have to get away from academic art of bourgeois taste, we have to reinvent nature. Nature should not be what we see, but what we want to see. So we create things in new colours, in new forms, we distort, we will remake a world that is more interesting to us." And then other people will see it that way. And then the same idea spreads through different countries and in different artistic disciplines. Now I find, because I have been teaching poetry, that I've started to write poetry again. I mean I had written two thousand poems maybe, all destroyed. I mean I could have gone around picking out a few of them in different magazines, collect them and so on, but I just decided no, that part of my life is finished. But now because I have to teach, I read and I explain and in the end suddenly I find late at night something comes to me and I mean not a little five line poem like this one that occurred to me in the middle of the night when I couldn't sleep, poems that are reflective, that bring in memory, that bring in observation, that make discoveries about the way the world is going and also close discoveries about myself and my awareness of getting older and all the dangers and hazards that are ahead of me the whole time.

going

F: You wrote a lot of obituaries. How many did you write so far?

C: I think about fifteen hundred.

F: What made you do that obituary business?

C: I was asked to. The paper rings you up, they say you know the person very well, would you write an obituary?

F: Where do you get the information? Do you have archives here?

C: I have a lot of archives here. Sometimes I interview people for their obituary. I don't tell them why, I say, "I will write an article about you." But...

F: But it will be published when you are dead.

C: I don't tell them that.

F: You have quite a reputation for writing obituaries in England. Are there people who refuse an interview with you because they think, maybe it's for my obituary?

C: No. (Looking through piles of papers) This is As and Bs. Here is Beckett's wife. I write obituaries for many different papers, I mean more for *The Independent* than anybody else, but also for *The Guardian*, *The Irish Times*, *The Scotsman*. I have done many publishers, of course, many writers, I do many musical people, politicians. And I think I'm doing them a service, it's a way of putting somebody in their place in history. Some time in the future, someone is going to come across that obituary and it will add a little bit to the history of that period. An obituary is important. Is the bottle already cold in there?

F: John, a last question. If we stick to your poem, we are now on going. Where to are you going?

C: Well I can only go one way: downward.

F: Downward?

C: Of course, I gradually fade out. My only fear about death is how I die. I would like to die with some dignity and today it is more difficult for people to die with dignity.

F: Do you think quite often of death?

C: Oh yes. I always have.

Interview: Walter Famler, Journalist, Publisher **Wespennest**
Translated from an interview in German from **Wespennest** *in 1996*

John Calder (Publishers) Limited

John Calder (Publishers) Limited
London: 1949-1964; 1975 -

Calder and Boyars
London: 1964 - 1975

John Calder (Publishers) Limited was started in 1949 to publish general quality literature and to fill the many gaps in current and classical literature created by wartime shortages. While at Zürich University studying political economy, John Calder had read European literature in the original languages. Returning to England, he found that many important works were out of print in English or had never been translated. Eighteenth and nineteenth century classics translated from the German, French, Italian, and Russian appeared in the firm's list together with new English and American novels and books on the arts, in particular music, opera, and drama. In 1958 Calder took a partner, Marion Boyars. The company's name was changed to Calder and Boyars in 1964; it was changed back in 1975 after the partnership broke up. Calder analyzed his forty years of publishing in his contribution to the 1989 – 1990 edition of *The Waterstone's Guide to Books:* "Creative literary publishing is totally different from general publishing and is more like running an art gallery. It needs the capital to endure a small and slow return, enough knowledge and energy to function effectively with little outside help, a small staff able to do anything and a missionary belief that the effort is worthwhile. It also needs a flair to publicize a personal taste so that the author one is trying to build up gets some benefit and recognition in his lifetime. Because a literary publisher starts with little competition, making his own discoveries, it is usually some time before he has to worry about larger, predatory publishers seducing is authors, and he must use that

35

MILLER

Henry Miller with a Calder & Boyars 1969 publication of Sexus

honeymoon period to get the confidence and affection of his writers. Then, provided he does his job well, he has a good chance of keeping his authors once they are established and profitable. He should also have the good luck to find at least one really unusual and important whose name will become synonymous with the imprint: this will give him the energy and pride to ride the waves of adversity that will inevitably attack him periodically."

In the mid 1950s Calder had found such a talent in Samuel Beckett, whom he would later describe as his "lucky genius, friend and guru." Calder also published the *nouveau roman* of Alain Robbe-Grillet, Nathalie Sarraute, Robert Pinget, Marguerite Duras, and Claude Simon; works by important German and Eastern European writers; and innovative novels by such British writers as Alan Burns, Aidan Higgins, Ann Quin, and Alexander Trocchi. Not all these writers have remained with Calder, for when the fourteen-year partnership with Boyars dissolved, she acquired half the list. During the partnership Calder and Boyars gained both profit and notoriety with works such as Henry Miller's *Tropic of Cancer* (1963) and *Tropic of Capricorn* (1964), as well as Herbert Selby's *Last Exit to Brooklyn* (1966). The latter was the subject of a much-publicized obscenity case at the Old Bailey. The company eventually won on appeal and reprinted twenty thousand copies of the book in response to widespread interest aroused by the case. As so often happens, the attempted suppression of the book only served to enhance its appeal for a larger public than it might otherwise have attracted. The firm is also noteworthy for having introduced absurdist theatre in the 1950s to Britain through the work of Eugene Ionesco, Fernando Arrabal, Pinget, Rene de Obaldia, and some British writers. There has been a continuing policy to publish British, American, and European plays, most notably the works of Howard Barker. The firm has also brought out expressionist and surrealist series of literature. As Calder expressed it in *The Waterstone's Guide To Books*, "Literature is an art, or should be: it is influenced by, and influences in its turn, the other arts." This view has led him into a deeper investigation of music, drama, philosophy, and politics, the result of which is an expanded list of books on these subjects and on related new ideas and critical approaches. Little by little he has abandoned general publishing in favour of what he calls "a more specialized list of books of and on literature and the related arts, with a large section devoted to opera."

– John Calder

The Writer's Champion

The Writer's Champion

Duncan Fallowell

meets Publisher of Genius John Calder as he embarks on his 45th year of literary adventure

John Calder is the hero of the adventure of literature. Throughout the Sixties, Calder & Boyars was by far the most interesting publishing house anywhere, its list overflowing with geniuses and eccentric talents – Pirandello, Wedekind, Marinetti, Borges, Pasolini, Artaud, Aragon, Breton, Michaux, Celine, Wyndham Lewis, Beckett, Miller, Burroughs, Ionesco, Kafka, the kings of 20th century literary daring.

The Calder enterprise was an extraordinary oxygen machine for the English-speaking world – the unexpected, the marvellous, the offensive found a place there – and alongside its translations of modernist European masterpieces and original works in English it included cultural magazines and important book series – The Opera Guides, Signature, European Classics, German Expressionism, French Surrealism. But it could be a risky business: Hubert Selby's *Last Exit to Brooklyn* was, in 1967, the last literary work to be seriously (though unsuccessfully) prosecuted for obscenity in the developed world – of course it was in England and of course it was a Calder book. At one point Calder had 18 Nobel prize-winners on his list, more than any other publisher, ever. And all from a creaky office in Soho.

This year marks 45 years in publishing for Mr. Calder but he began early – he will be 67 on 25 January. Today he has offices in Paris and New York as well as London and it would be nice to call this an empire. But it isn't. 'These are very difficult times,' he asserts. He says everything assertively. His three offices are each a single room with a telephone, filing cabinet, bookstack.

39

Ousted from Soho, the London office is currently on the first floor of an early 19th century house situated where King's Cross, Bloomsbury and Clerkenwell lose themselves in each other. A dank, drizzly Sunday afternoon finds Calder at a desk here, poring over columns of figures with a tight mouth. Not surprisingly, his latest book series is *World in Crisis.*

John Calder was born in Ayrshire into a Scottish family involved in the manufacture of alcoholic drinks. His background rapidly became cosmopolitan. Evacuated to Canada in 1940 by his French-Canadian mother, he went to McGill University. After the war his stepfather advised him to become a banker, so he returned to Europe and attended the University of Zurich.

Calder inherited a little money on his father's death in 1944, and in 1950 started up his own publishing house with 500 pounds and a partner in the basement off Belgrave Square. He began by publishing war books, followed by translations of works by classic Europeans – Tolstoy, Chekhov, Goethe, - previously unavailable in English. Then he started to publish a lot of American books which during the McCarthy era could not be published in the US. Then in the mid Fifties, he discovered Samuel Beckett.

'I went to see *Waiting for Godot* and was puzzled by it, so I went to see it again and got what I'd missed the first time around. I wrote to Beckett's French publisher but it went to the wrong address and Faber got in ahead of me, got Godot with an option on everything else. But they decided the novels were obscene and unpublishable, so Beckett wrote to me and I took the fiction and the poetry. Now we have 80 per cent of Beckett's writings.

'Sam hated people who just wanted to meet him because he was famous. He was also incredibly generous and had qualities which today might almost be considered saintly. Total lack of greed or personal ambition. In the late Fifties and Sixties I saw him about once a month and we never went to bed until dawn. We'd go around playing ping-pong, billiards, chess in cafes – you can do this all night in Paris.'

'Do you still stay up until dawn?'

'No. I have to work 90 to 100 hours a week.' Indeed, John Calder's days are more hectic and gruelling than ever. He rises between 5am and 6am and writes for a couple of hours, mainly journalism. 'If I'm in Paris, which I shall be tonight, I teach Monday to Wednesday and back in London Wednesday night–'

JOHN MINIHAN

Calder&Ionesco

John Calder and Eugene Ionesco

'Teach?'

'Yes, it's a new activity. Thursdays and Fridays I go round the bookshops – I fired all the reps, had to – I've been doing bookshops this week in Edinburgh, Durham, Newcastle, and that was combined with a BBC broadcast in Edinburgh, then giving a talk to the Scottish Arts Club, debating at Durham University Friday night. And last night I saw *Tristan and Isolde* in Newcastle-'

'What do you teach?'

'French and English literature at a school in Paris, which gives me a French income and puts me in the French social security system – the security system here is collapsing.'

'And you prefer Paris?'

'Yes, people are alive there, discussing ideas. Cultural life in Britain has almost disappeared.'

'You mean swallowed up by commercialism?'

He sighs, but quickly. He does everything quickly. 'Yes, and as a result the literary scene in London is dull, shallow, Philistine. Very few English or American books have any literary content whatsoever. Literary editors hardly know anything about literature, they just want to go to parties. If you write a book about a scandal in the royal family they're all over you. Otherwise they're just not interested.'

'But your own journalism...'

'I write obituaries for *The Independent.*'

'Who are they of?'

'Of those which appeared last year – Jean-Louis Barrault, Ionesco...'

'Oh was he difficult?'

'Ionesco was very difficult. His fame – he didn't really believe it – he felt it was a dream he was going to wake up from and be back teaching school at a Paris suburb wondering how to pay the rent. His general paranoia meant that he had no sense of loyalty to anyone at all.'

'Were many of your writers difficult?'

'So many of them were. Marguerite Duras – we'd published her novels, film scripts, plays, without much success – she left me for Collins the moment she had a bestseller, *The Lover.* I rang her up and said Marguerite, this is not the way to treat me after all I've done for you," and she said, "I don't care about that, I don't owe anything to anybody, adieu."'

'Did you enjoy the Sixties?'

'Enormously! Everything seemed to go right.'

In the Seventies, Calder tried to branch out. He contested, as a Liberal, two Scottish parliamentary constituencies as well as the European parliamentary seat for central Scotland. Thrice he was unelected.

'If you go into politics you have to really want to be elected in which case you temper what you say to what people want to hear. I, however, told them what I felt they ought to hear.'

'You have this didactic side.'

'I've always had an interest in trying to improve the world, in making the best available to more people. Then came the horror of horrors – Margaret Thatcher – and in 15 years she put the country back a century in social deprivation, Philistinism, the old class attitudes.'

The heat of a muted but constant rage can be sensed behind a great deal of Calder's conversation, but the Thatcher revolution seems to have had its effect on him in more subtle ways too. When I last saw him it was in the Seventies in Brewer Street, he was wearing a corduroy jacket and greenish open-necked shirt. Now he's in a white collar and tie and striped navy blue suit, the banker emerging at last.

Otherwise he looks hardly any older – the same round face and thinning hair, the same compact Jack Russell demeanour and air of applied energy. He never looks one in the eye for more than a second.

Occasionally he smiles, and one is delighted by it, coming as it does out of this buttoned-down ferocity.

At its height, the Brewer Street office of Calder & Boyars employed 17 people. But Calder and Marion Boyars fell out and went their separate ways, and as the Eighties advanced John increasingly felt the chill. A small clause in the Brewer Street lease obliged him to spend 80,000 pounds on the wretched building – the money wasn't exactly lying around, before vacating it in 1989. He fell behind on royalty payments to, for example, William Burroughs, whom he'd been publishing courageously since 1962, and lost the rights to Burroughs's books.

'Does this sort of thing make you bitter?'

'Sometimes. But on the other hand I think life is a rather bad joke. Nothing really matters in the long run. Beckett who was a good friend, someone I miss very much, terribly loyal, did a lot to help my thinking in that direction. He said when you get older you must learn to discard things because things are going to discard you.'

'And how do you see your future in the coming years?'

'The coming years? I think in weeks. The reason I've got these figures out here on the desk is because there's not enough money to pay the bills and I've got to decide what to pay where, how to talk to them. I'm not paying myself anything right now.'

Who was it who said a man must choose between wealth and glory in this life? Well, John Calder has made no money out of it – and no honours either in his own country. But in France he is twice a Chevalier and his record as a publisher is the most glorious of his generation. That doesn't pay the bills but, as literature makes its stand against consumerism in the eternal struggle between quality and quantity, it is something for every literate man and woman to remember on Mr. Calder's birthday.

© *The Observer Review*, *January 5, 1995*

THE NOUVEAU ROMAN READER

NATHALIE SARRAUTE

CLAUDE SIMON

MARGUERITE DURAS

ALAIN ROBBE-GRILLET

CLAUDE MAURIAC

ROBERT PINGET

MICHEL BUTOR

JEAN RICARDOU

EDITED BY

JOHN FLETCHER & JOHN CALDER

JOHN MINIHAN

❝ *Anything about Princess Diana, for example, will get reviewed. But serious books by serious writers have great difficulty in getting noticed.* **❞**

– *John Calder*

The Last of the Gentleman Publishers

The Last of the Gentleman Publishers

Baret Magarian

*F*or the past half-century John Calder's name has been synonymous with literary excellence. He began in 1949, publishing foreign and political titles, and acquiring a reputation for taking books that others wouldn't go near.

Things took off in 1963 when he published Henry Miller's sexually explicit *Tropic of Cancer*. It sold 40,000 and Calder was able to print all the manuscripts that had until then been gathering dust. During the sixties he joined forces with Marion Boyars, and together they published the most interesting fiction and drama around: Borges, Artaud, Burroughs, Celine, Pasolini, Miller, Ionesco, Beckett, Breton, and Pirandello. Calder was the first to introduce Britain to the practitioners of the *nouveau roman*, principally Claude Simon, Alain Robbe-Grillet and Nathalie Sarraute. Over the years he has had 18 Noble Prizewinners on his list, more than any other publisher.

Next year will mark his 50th year in publishing. But times are hard. He has managed to retain a distinguished set of writers, most notably Samuel Beckett, Celine and Howard Barker, but he lost many when he was unable to keep up on royalty payments. This was a direct result of the loss of his Arts Council grant in 1983. Marguerite Duras, Henry Miller, and William Burroughs were all plucked up by other publishers.

As we talk in his London office his determined gaze and clipped accent create an air of stoicism.

"The then literature committee of the Arts Council, under the Conservatives, was taken over by people who didn't know anything about serious literature. They said the books we published were no longer of any interest, even though in 1985 Claude Simon won the Nobel Prize, Howard Barker the Italia Prize for best radio play and Barbara Wright the Scott Moncrieff prize for best translation."

Calder Publications now finds itself in a unique position as the last of the independent publishers. This means he isn't owned by anyone else, and does not have to answer to anyone else. "We are also one of the few publishers that still carries the flag for the English language, which is in great danger of disappearing under the American vernacular, because British books are increasingly being edited by American editors."

John Calder's activities are a myriad. He is not only a publisher, but an editor, translator, journalist, and critic (a book on Beckett's philosophy is due later this year). In addition, he has just kick-started a national campaign to draw attention to the arts in this country.

"Societies without the arts lack the critical edge that enables people to see through bad administrators and governments, and as a result they are always under demagogues and dictators.

"We need to make the Government realize the importance of the arts, which is why I'm involved in a National Rally for the Arts, which will take place on 1 and 2 May 1999 in Hyde Park.

"We're hoping to get as many as a million people to go, when there will be free entertainment by theatre companies, bands, orchestras, artists of every kind.

"We want to get the Government positively on the side of the arts, and get more funding for them. No country in Europe has the arts at such a low level as they are in this country. And I think Tony Blair will have a sort of miraculous conversion when he realizes he'll be losing votes if he doesn't start to do something."

The conversation shifts from a moral agenda to an anecdotal one. I ask him about Beckett, whom he met in the 1950s, gaining the right to his fiction when Faber refused to take it, considering it too difficult.

"Beckett was actually a very simple person in almost every way. He got on well with any normal, natural person, but he couldn't stand lion hunters. He was really the ideal author, extremely punctilious, and extremely loyal. He had a very caustic wit. I remember going to Lords with him and the critic Harold Hobson. Hobson said: 'On a day like this you feel glad to be alive.' There was a pause and then Beckett said; 'Well I wouldn't go as far as that.'"

What do you think of literary fiction today? "I'm sure there are very good things being written, even getting published, but the problem is they aren't getting reviewed. Even when you get a literary editor who would like to review serious books he's not allowed to. His job depends on getting reviews of topical books. Anything about Princess Diana, for example, will get reviewed. But serious books by serious writers have great difficulty in getting noticed. And editors at publishing houses are now completely under the thumb of the management, which is accountant-controlled. For an editor to discover a new, exciting author will cut no ice with an editorial board dominated by accountants who only want to know how many copies the books sell."

Calder thinks that we may see more independent publishers starting up to counter this. One hopes that someone with his determination and willingness to take risks will come along.

This determination extends to acting as his own representative with the booksellers. This, combined with going to conferences, working in his Paris and London offices, and writing, adds up to a marathon 100-hour working week for him.

But why can't he get someone else to sell the books?

"None of the reps was willing to find out what the books were about! I found I achieved more in a day than they did in three months."

What about the future of the list? "I've no more idea of the future of the list than I have about my own future. I would like to think that someone would come along and carry it on, someone willing to put in the dedication, to work that 100 hours for extremely little return."

John Calder turned 71 this year. In France he has been made a Chevalier twice. In Britain he has received no public honours. He is neither surprised nor dismayed by this. But for those who care about serious literature his career embodies the defiant intelligence and excellence that is its hallmark.

From *The Wednesday Review*, *The Independent* 24 June, 1998

AMY LAND

John Calder has attended over 3000 performances of 800 different operas!

He records the details of every single performance he attends in the above five volumes of opera diaries.

Alannah Hopkin

It sounded too bizarre to be true: the publisher John Calder had been spotted in Cork, then in Dublin, then in Sligo, doing the rounds of the bookshops with his catalogue, taking orders. Rumours about Calder, the publisher of Samuel Beckett among others, abound. Was this yet another embroidery on the myth?

The last I had heard was that his company had gone bankrupt in the UK, and that he himself had emerged, phoenix-like from the ashes, and was living in some splendour in Paris.

This turned out to be only partly true (he denies the splendour), while the original story of this fabled 70-year-old publisher and editor footslogging around the country's bookshops is wholly true.

John Calder is a small, tense man, initially suspicious of strangers. I have known him very slightly for 15 years or so. When I lived in Soho, an amiable American ran Calder's one-room office, and when the boss was away, a gang of us used it as a quiet refuge if the pub got too noisy. There was an enormous floor-to-ceiling bookcase which contained samples of the numerous titles that Calder had in print.

It was both an education and a journey in nostalgia to browse around it. Besides Beckett's prose, including *Murphy* and the trilogy, there were the French *nouveau roman* crowd – Alain Robbe-Grillet, Nathalie Sarraute, Marguerite Duras – diverse modern classics such as Celine's *Journey to the End of the Night,* Jorge Luis Borges' *Fictions,* William Burroughs's *The Naked Lunch*, Aidan Higgins's *Langrishe, Go Down*, and many many more.

DAVID APPLEFIELD

66 *...I asked John to supper. He turned up with not one, but three bottles of good wine.* **99**

— *Alannah Hopkin*

Aidan Higgins (who happens to be my husband) is one of several people to repeat stories of John Calder's legendary generosity as a host, while complaining of his equally legendary tight-fistedness when it comes to paying out royalties. Aidan was recommended to Calder by Beckett, and Calder published both *Felo da Se*, and his first collection of stories in 1959, and then *Langrishe, Go Down*, which went on to win the James Tait Black Memorial Prize. With Boswell-like brilliance, Calder edited both books line by line, and when Aidan was struggling with the *Balcony of Europe*, Calder worked with him daily for a year to reduce the massive typescript to a 463 page book, which was eventually shortlisted for the Booker Prize.

When I caught up with Calder during his annual two-week sales trip, in the course of which he visits some 150 bookshops, he revealed that he was still selling the hardback *Balcony of Europe*, both here and in America.

After a pleasant discussion of the history of Calder Publications, I asked him to supper. He turned up with not one, but three bottles of good wine.

So why, said Aidan, who does not hesitate to mix business with pleasure, have I not had a royalty cheque from you for over 15 years...

This is a simplified version of Calder's story: born into a well-off family in Perth Scotland, as a young man he was sent to Zurich to study economics. During his stay abroad he also discovered literature, theatre and opera (such is his devotion to the latter that he has recently attended his 800th performance). When he went to London to work in a timber company, he shared a flat with a man who persuaded him to go into publishing. He waived most of his commission as a salesman to become a company director, and when the timber company was taken over in 1957, he was able to go into publishing full-time.

Calder is fluent in French and German and has some Russian. Initially he began doing new editions of European classics such as Chekhov, Goethe and Stendhal. He approached Samuel Beckett on the strength of *Waiting for Godot*, and made contact one day after Faber had secured the rights to Beckett's plays. Faber thought the prose works were probably obscene, and did not know what to do with them, which is how they fell to Calder.

In those days Beckett was referred to as "Calder's Folly." He printed 3,000 copies of *Malone Dies* and sold only about 200 in the first year. The Nobel Prize helped, as did academia's discovery of Beckett, but only recently has Calder managed to get Beckett into Eason's which he considers a significant advance.

The Arts Council in the UK had been helping with subsidies on individual books since the early 70s. It offered an annual grant if he would make the company into a trust, which he did. Then, in the Thatcher years, Lord Rees-Mogg was made chairman of the Arts Council and simply cut Calder off the list. The best option was to declare the company bankrupt.

In contrast, the French Ministry of Culture was keen to employ John Calder on an ad-hoc basis; hence the move to Paris. Calder claims that he makes no money at all out of publishing. His personal income comes from journalism, chiefly obituary-writing for the *Guardian* and the *London Independent*. He reckons he holds some kind of record, having written to date almost 3,000 obituaries.

The reason he is on the road selling his own books is simply because he is good at it and can find nobody else to do it. He also makes regular sales trips to Australia, New Zealand, Canada and the US. He still has about 500 titles in print, most of which he believes would disappear if Calder Publications ceased to exist.

The company is still a charity, a trust, and Calder is looking at ways of getting it endowed to keep it going after his time. He would like it to go on, but it is proving hard to find someone who (a) has the same sort of editorial talent, and (b) is also a dedicated salesperson, willing to do the hard slog for little or no pay.

Any takers?

*From **The Irish Times**, 1997*

section three

section three

III

JOHN CALDER
1986

SAMUEL
BECKETT ❯

at
80
NOBEL
PRIZE ⟫⟫
1969

◀ CLAUDE
SIMON

NOBEL
PRIZE
1985

Remise des insignes d'officier de l'ordre national du merite a John Calder

Jean Gueguinou
Ambassador of France to Great Britain

What more fitting setting in which to pay tribute to you, *mon cher* John Calder, than here, in the midst of your friends, at the French Institute? And on what better occasion than the traditional presentation of the Scott Moncrieff prize, dedicated to the art of translation? - Pay tribute to you on your elevation to the rank of *Officier* in our National Order of Merit.

"Superior quality," "excellence," two definitions of the word "merit" – both are wholly applicable in your case. In celebrating your achievements, we are saluting the man who, over the years, has been the greatest publisher of French literature in the UK.

You have no equal in the history of British publishing and, I fear, alas, we are unlikely to see many, if any, in the future. What you have done is genuinely unique, amazing: your services to literature and the circulation of ideas, your energetic battles against all attempts to trivialize the written word, or, purely and simply, commercialize it.

You are modest, but your catalogue speaks for you. And it's very talkative! Among the writers you published in their youth, let me pick out just a few: Beckett, of course - and how enduring that association has been – Aragon, Claude Simon, Queneau, le Clezio, Breton, Robbe-Grillet, Sarraute, Duras, Celine, Mandiargues, Adamov...what a list! It alone is enough to give an inferiority complex to any young British publisher trying to emulate your example. Those young writers have become great classical authors. Perhaps indeed, as Joubert maintained, "the only great drawback of new books is that they prevent us

JOHN MINIHAN

66 I thought it important for France to recognize your achievements in the battle you have been waging doggedly over these past fifteen years. 99

— Jean Gueguinou

from reading the old ones," and that's why, intimidated, British publishers no longer, or only very rarely, publish the works of young French writers...

But that's not the real reason. The real reason is that every generation isn't lucky enough to have a John Calder.

Admittedly you had a propitious start in life: a Canadian mother, a Scottish father, that's an excellent launch pad for a Francophone and Francophile like you. But to go from there, to becoming *the* publisher of French literature in the United Kingdom, and *so French* that your offices are now in France, nevertheless required a huge educational and cultural leap.

A life devoted to literature and translation, and the last bastion of independent publishing in this country. Indeed, "Copyright" last year's Franco-British Book Fair, held right here in the Institute, paid glowing tribute to your achievements, and stubborn determination to safeguard both independence and standards. Many distinguished members of the Franco-British literary fraternity were involved in the Fair, and I had the pleasure of hosting a reception for them at the Residency, at which, appropriately enough, I presented the insignia of the *Ordre des Arts et Lettres* to Dame Muriel Spark, Sir Vidiadhar Naipaul and Terry Hale. You, *cher* John, are already a member of that Order, and already a *Chevalier de l'Ordre du Merite*, a distinction awarded to you back in '83. But that's a long time ago and I thought it important for France to recognize your achievements since then, in the battle you have been waging doggedly over these past fifteen years. She is doing so this evening.

These fifteen years have, I know, been particularly difficult. Deprived of a previously substantial State subsidy, your publishing house has succeeded, against all the odds, in fighting off takeovers and mergers. What indeed would Calder Publications Ltd. be without John Calder? You were also, incidentally, one of the rare publishers to go to the High Court to defend the Net Book Agreement, citing the French example in support of your argument.

But I know too that, over this period, you have also had the pleasure of writing and publishing the famous ENO Opera Guides, of seeing hundreds of opera performances, and enjoying the gastronomic delights of French cuisine while remaining loyal to your London club, which, by the way, has nothing English about it, since it's the Caledonian...

Tonight, in this building you know well, and in which I like to think you feel at home, I wanted to pay you this tribute and encourage you to keep up your good work, go on being what you are. As the great Franco-American novelist, Julian Green, wrote in his "Journal": by dint of regularity announcing the death of the book, we have, finally ended up by recognizing that it is eternal. Let us all wish John Calder Publications, if perhaps not immorality, then certainly a very long and successful life!

Institut Français, 8 December 1997

Calder vs. The Old Boys

Bill Webb

The late Fifties - to be precise- 1959 - when John Calder began his career as a full-time publisher, and I began to edit the *Guardian's* book pages from the paper's old home in Cross Street, Manchester, was a strange sort of time. The postwar world was properly under way at last, the suppression of the Hungarian Uprising having disabused all but the most of the brainwashed of the notion of pas d'enemis a gauche, and the Suez debacle curing any remaining follies of imperial grandeur, at least until Madame Thatcher so disastrously reinfected half of the nation. Colin MacInnes had written the first of his reconnaissances of the arriving youth culture, and the Beatles were just over the horizon, but there were also cultural lags or continuities which seem even more extraordinary as one looks back on them now.

Some of these were simply the physical continuings that made for a living contact not just with the pre-war world but with the world before the first World War and the beginnings of Bloomsbury, whose doings and writings cast a lengthening and rather discouraging shade over English literary culture. E.M. Forster was still alive, T.S. Eliot was sometimes to be seen in the offices of Faber & Faber, Bertrand Russell, as well as leading the anti-nuclear Committee of 100, was writing his lengthy and absorbing memoirs, as was Leonard Woolf. In the publishing world, going to Victor Gollancz still meant dealing with Victor himself, Hamish Hamilton ran Hamish Hamilton, and Billy Collins was William Collins personified. The almost Victorian figure of Stanley Unwin remained in charge of Allen & Unwin, and there

were Macmillans conning the books at Macmillans yet, while not only
was that tough old dandy Frederic Warburg in the chair at Secker &
Warburg, but Martin Secker himself, Lawrence's first publisher, was
still producing books on fin de siècle themes from his office in Covent
Garden. The small Viennese invasion – George Weidenfeld, Andre
Deutsch, Paul Elek – had consolidated itself. The great American
Conquest, which by the mid 90s would leave the merest handful of
significant London publishing houses not owned and controlled by
transatlantic conglomerates, was as yet unimagined and unimaginable
(though most of the books that mattered most in the 1959 season -
Saul Bellow's *Henderson the Rain King*, Lowell's *Life Studies*, and
Richard Ellmann's state-of-the-art critical biography of James Joyce -
were by American writers).

What made me notice the arrival of John Calder and his lists, both
personally and professionally, was first his passionate devotion to the
work and person of Samuel Beckett, whose strange music the actor
Patrick Magee had introduced me to some years earlier in Ireland.
(Another friend, Tim O'Keeffe, at MacGibbon and Kee, had begun to
put the heart back into Joyce's other great Irish heir Flann O'Brien, a
rescue operation without which *At Swim-Two-Birds* would probably
been recovered too late, and we should never have had *The Third
Policeman* or his other 'misterpieces'. Typically, Tim and the better
part of his list were victims of one of the first of many destructive
publishing takeovers to come.) I suppose Faber, who had cornered
Beckett's plays, might eventually have done the underprized prose
fiction, though someone there - Eliot? Charles Monteith? - had decided
that *Malone Dies* was obscene, but it would be hard to imagine anyone,
unless perhaps O'Keeffe, matching John's championing of the novels
and his dedicated perseverance with the *unheimlich* boneyard gleam
of the intense, short last pieces. What was otherwise unmistakable
about him and his list was the knowledge they showed of the world
of literatures beyond the Anglo-American pale, and their lack of interest,
by and large, in the conservative and comfortable domesticity of much
English fiction of the time. As for the Americans he published -
Burroughs, Henry Miller, Hubert Selby's *Last Exit to Brooklyn*, for which
he fought three heroic cases in the courts, finally winning on appeal,
with the help of John Mortimer's commentary - they were hardly the
approved orthodoxy. (When he was still a part-time publisher, not
yet released from the family timber firm, he had specialised in bringing
out here the American casualties of McCarthyism.)

The most significant shift in writing in Britain since the war had been that loose alliance against both the social and cultural snobbery of the Oxbridge-Bloomsbury axis and the rather anaemic strain of surrealism in English poetry of the Forties. 'The Movement', as it allowed itself ironically to be known, was launched, improbably as that seems now, in a radio magazine, edited by John Wain, and revolved around the taste and talents of Philip Larkin and Kingsley Amis and their friends, a group of writers as distinctly representative of their movement in the fifties as Auden, Spender and Isherwood had been in the thirties. *I Like It Here* was the programmatic title of Amis' second novel, and the poems of Larkin and Donald Davie were as assertive, in their different ways, of the texture and authenticity of English provincial life, and, though none was particuarly interested in formal politics, of the more democratic tone in English culture. It was, I suppose, a belated part of the modest postwar political revolution in Britain, bringing both culture and society a bit more up to date and closer together.

But by the end of the decade what was most beneficial about this peculiarly English modernisation had had its effect, and even for some of the people who had been part of it or enthusiastic about it, cultural life in England was beginning to feel narrow, monochrome, more than a little claustrophobic: "Fog in Channel: Continent Cut Off", as the old joke about insularity had it. My particular point of embarkation was found in another ground-breaking radio series, eventually edited into a book with the title *Under Pressure*, in which A. Alvarez, a poet and critic also connected with 'The Movement', introduced us to the stoic and subtle writers of a forgotten Eastern Europe, whose great cities, with their fertile cultural history, had been lost in the icy fogs of the cold war. Soon I was able to read and write about some of them - Zbigniew Herbert, the Czech Holub, the Hungarians of two brilliant generations, all published in the invaluable *Modern European Poets* series Nikos Stangos edited for Penguin Books - and reflect on what Ted Hughes had written in an introduction to the work of their Yugoslav contemporary Vasko Popa: "These are not the spoiled brats of (Western) civilisation disappointed of impossible and unreal expectations and deprived off the revelations of necessity."

John's contribution to the widening of British cultural horizons was of several kinds. First, he introduced reluctant British reviewers to Alain Robbe-Grillet, Nathalie Sarraute, Duras and other French novelists of the Nouvelle Vague (which is not to forget his nurturing also of Barbara Wright's marvellous translations of Raymond Queneau). Then, as well as the early novel Heinrich Boll, he brought out editions of that classic German literature which had been wiped off the English cultural map by the propaganda and prejudices that inevitably accompanied two world wars and that remain deeply rooted still. He was the only native head of a British publishing firm who had been educated largely abroad - at Zurich and McGill. He spoke French and German fluently, and enough Italian and Spanish to make his way at the Frankfurt Book Fair.

There were other consequences of this liberation from the conventional education of his British class. One was a taste for a kind of *avant-garde* lark that sometimes make things happen. There are endless newspaper cuttings from the Sixties and Seventies about the high-voltage literary festivals he organized at the Edinburgh Festival and elsewhere, including inevitably the 'happening' involving the trundling of a naked beauty through the hall in a wheelbarrow that shocked the socks off the Wee Frees. Also well-remembered is the Harrogate Festival of 1969, when the local CID made nervous inquiries about the possible arrival from California of a certain Professor Marcuse, perhaps fearing a neo-Marxist uprising of the Spa's ardent youth.

It was a time, we had both felt in the Fifties, when the book-reading part of Middle England needed some persuading that concerns for literature and politics weren't mutually exclusive (nor need wordmen be musically literate, music especially opera, being another realm in which John was also unEnglishly ardent, both in his life and his publishing). As to politics, it wasn't just that in several elections in the Seventies he was to stand as a parliamentary candidate for the Liberals, seeing (more prophetically than one realized at the time) an essential conservatism in both the other machine-run parties. I'm thinking rather of his serious early involvement in the Committee of 100 and the fact that it was John who was responsible for making us know about what the French were actually doing in Algeria by translating (in a day and a half) Henri Alleg's searing book about the army's use of torture in that savagely reluctant retreat from empire.

"He has a finger in so many pies," wrote a bemused interviewer in 1962, "that he often seems to be a refugee from Alice in Wonderland." But it was uphill work, unstuffing the Brits. There were exceptions like O'Keefe and Tom Maschler and Peter Owen, who also cared about the kind of writing that changed the way you saw the world and didn't bridle at authors with funny foreign names but there was certainly

DAVID APPLEFIELD

Calder & Wagenbach

John Calder and Klaus Wagenbach
with a book by the poet Erich Fried

somthing in what John said about British publishing at the time he came into it: that it was run by two kinds of old men, the old ones and the young ones.

Now, on gloomy days, one might say that it's by two kinds of accountant, British and increasingly the American. And still John Calder is there fighting his corner, fighting for literature and for the freedom of the word without which all other freedoms cannot even be articulated. In a cold week in January this year - 1997- it wasn't any of the managerial elite of British Publishing Inc. who stood alone in the High Court unrepresented by expensive counsel, to demonstrate how the Net Book Agreement was likely to cripple most small independent publishers and booksellers, but the same stocky Aberdeen Angus bull of a man, improbably seventy now, charging a British establishment more concerned with profit than with publishing the best that's known or thought.

John's own rallying cry on bad days has long been Beckett's particularly tonic injunction to, "Fail again. Fail better." His own front list is sadly truncated these days, but the backlist - which before the hard times of the Eighties and Nineties included no less than 18 Nobel Prizewinners - is incomparable: a formidable reminder of the worlds we should have lost without him.

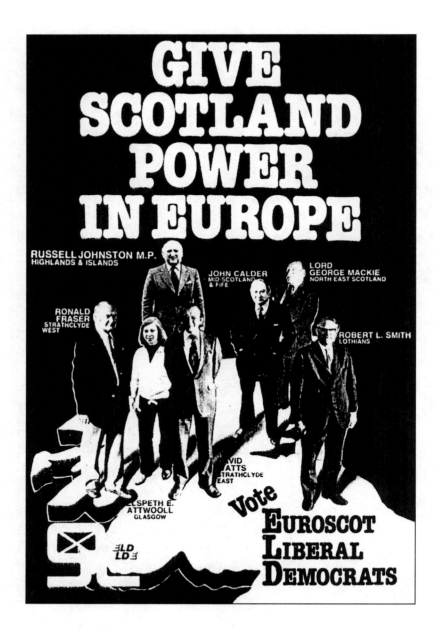

John Calder:
Scottish Impresario
& Scottish Liberal Politician

Richard Beith

My wife, Margaret, and I moved from the south of England to central Scotland in the late summer of 1966. As far as our concert and opera going activities were concerned, this meant that we exchanged the Royal Opera, Covent Garden, the then Sadler's Wells Opera and concerts at London's Royal Festival Hall, for the Scottish National Orchestra (not yet Royal), the splendours of Scottish Opera, then coming into its golden period and the world-wide musical variety to be found every summer at the Edinburgh International Festival. Not a bad swap; we soon heard about an additional bonus.

This was a modest, but fascinating, institution called *Ledlanet Nights*. Conceived as a smaller scale Scottish country version of the famous Glyndbourne Opera in Sussex, it featured performances of opera, orchestral and chamber concerts, plays and folk songs. Ledlanet was the name of a Victorian shooting lodge, near Milnathort, Kinrossshire, which a certain John Calder had inherited from his great uncle, Sir James Calder, in 1962. John had visited this family home on many previous occasions and, as he was often working in Edinburgh, in connection with literary conferences for the Festival, he decided to make use of this asset and to found:

A new kind of festival, one where enjoyment combines with instruction and where conviviality plays a large part in the creation of atmosphere.

– Scottish Opera Magazine, Autumn 1966

The main architectural feature of the building was a central ground floor hall with a splendid double staircase leading to a gallery, the whole well suited to dramatic use and with a side room off the hall which could be used by the orchestra during operatic performances. The seating was *not* Victorian, just basic trestles with a plentitude of scaffolding to support the upper layers. Nevertheless, the setting worked very well and there was always the 75 minute dinner interval between Act 1 and Act 2 or the two parts of a concert, in which one could stretch, eat and imbibe. The lodge was located in the Ochil Hills, so the drive up to the house and the interval walks in the grounds were set in some of the most unspoilt scenery in Central Scotland.

The number of seats for the audience was progressively raised from 80 in 1963 to 120 and eventually to 159. The catering facilities were improved so that a three-course interval dinner could be eaten in comfort and a regular band of staff and volunteer helpers was re-cruited. Frequent visitors soon began to know Attewell, the butler/ maitre d' figure, Jock, the barman and, of course, John Calder himself as kilted host. Performances were divided up between four or so short seasons per year, with a particular emphasis on rare operas. The Ledlanet seasons continued through the late 1960s, eventually coming to an end in 1973 when a major and expensive refurbishment of the house would have been required to allow continuation of the use as a place of public entertainment. There was an even more ambitious plan at that time, with a brand new theatre of 600 seats in the grounds with a sunken orchestra pit à la Bayreuth and with the old house being used solely for eating and drinking. Alas, that was not to be though detailed plans were drawn up.

What works, what artists were typical of a Ledlanet season? The early years featured mainly small-scale works, sung by such well-known performers as Josephine Veasey, Geraint Evans and Ian Wallace. When full operas were given, John cast them from the ranks of up and coming singers, often current members of the Covent Garden or Glyndbourne Chorus. One particular Ledlanet theme was the pro-duction of staged or semi-staged versions of works normally performed in the concert hall, certainly not in costume. The critics didn't always agree with this policy but interesting productions were given of Janacek's the *Diary of a Young Man Who Disappeared*, Britten's Can-ticle *Abraham and Isaac*, Schoenberg's *Pierrot Lunaire* and even Schumann's *Dichterleibe*. Memorable opera productions included *Alcina, Parthenope* and *Agrippina* by Handel, *The Turn of the Screw* by Benjamin Britten, *Una Cosa Rara* by Martin y Soler, Mozart's *La*

Clemenza di Tito, Il Re Pastore and *Idomeneo,* Gluck's *Alceste,* and Humperdink's *Hansel and Gretel.*

The acceptance of many young singers was accelerated by their appearance at Ledlanet. Names that spring to mind include Josephine Barstow, Jill Gomez, Philip Langridge, Sandra Browne and Denis O'Neill. Neither was drama neglected in Ledlanet's twelve seasons. One of the most fondly remembered productions combined music and drama in a unique way. In April 1970 John presented his own exploration of the life and music of Beethoven in honour of the Beethoven Bicentenary. The text was adapted from Beethoven's own writings and those of his contemporaries. Leonard Maguire was the narrator, a string quartet led by Leonard Friedman played quartet movements and that fine actor Patrick Wymark played the part of Beethoven. Sadly, this was the last part that Patrick was to play on a British stage. Art exhibitions were also held to coincide with festival seasons; artists included the late Nicholas Fairbairn QC, later a local MP and the irrepressible Richard Demarco.

The Autumn 1973 Season proved to be the last public performance at Ledlanet; *Idomeneo* was its swansong except for a small Christmas season given in Kinross Town hall. The proposed new theatre was never built, but in those twelve seasons John Calder and his team brought live theatre and live music of all kinds to Kinross-shire and to a wider audience. They revived unjustly neglected works, helped promote new performing talent and left their audiences feeling that they had been part of something special.

My wife was a member of the then (English) Liberal Party by conviction, I was a later convert but we had both been modestly involved in Party activity in the 1964 and 1966 British General Elections. Moving to live in central Scotland we assumed that the hills of Perthshire (where we then lived) would be covered in active Liberals. This was a slightly optimistic view, but enough good Scottish Liberals such as Margaret Begg and Alan Clark of Crieff came together in our Parliamentary Constituency, then called Kinross and West Perthshire, for the local Liberal Association to be revived and the decision taken to fight the seat at the forthcoming General Election. However, to fight an election, it is best to have a candidate, so, apart from publicity and fundraising our chief concern was to find such a person. By this time it was early 1970 and Margaret and I had been enjoying Ledlanet Nights for a good three years and had got to know John Calder on a conversational basis. We deduced that he was a liberal (lower case 'l') but

IMEC ARCHIVES

66 Campaigning with John was great fun;
he was an enthusiast for the cut and
thrust of politics at a local level and was
happy speaking at the numerous villages
and small towns... 99

– *Richard Beith*

was he a Liberal or rather, a Scottish Liberal with an uppercase "L"? Our committee, of which I was Hon. Secretary at the time, decided to ask John to be our candidate for Parliament. After some thought, John agreed. So, we had an interesting candidate with a home, Ledlanet, within our Constituency.

The General Election came in June 1970, blessed (?) with beautiful weather. Campaigning with John was great fun; he was an enthusiast for the cut and thrust of politics at a local level and was happy speaking at the numerous villages and small towns which made up this very rural constituency. With his many connections John was able to provide guest speakers such as the actor Patrick Wymark (see Beethoven above). Excellent actor that he was, he still had to be taught lines such as: *It doesn't matter who you vote for as long as you don't vote Conservative* were not quite what was required and that the idea was to persuade people to vote *for* John and the Liberal cause. However Patrick didn't need to be taught that feudalism still thrived in Conservative Perthshire. Canvassing for John one day near Dunkeld he asked to be allowed to address a group of farm workers; *Go ahead,* said the farmer, *you can talk to them but they'll vote the way I tell them.*

Polling Day came and went and at the count next morning the sitting Conservative MP, Sir Alec Douglas-Home, was duly sent back to Westminster, with the Labour, Liberal and Scottish Nationalist candidates trailing behind him. *Was it worth it?*, we said as we all sat around a lunch in Perth after the declaration. Of course it was; the most important aspect echoed in a letter of appreciation received from a Church Minister was that John and his campaign team had given Liberal sympathizers the chance to vote for what they believed in and not have to use their vote for a second-best choice.

John was later re-adopted as prospective Liberal candidate for Kinross and West Perthshire, but had to resign this position in the mid-seventies to concentrate on his business interests. However, as an international publisher, he was a obvious choice to represent the Liberal case when Great Britain participated in the first direct elections to the European Parliament in the summer of 1979. European constituencies are enormous in size and *Mid-Scotland and Fife* was no exception. However meetings were held, phone-in times publicized and countless press releases issued. John's commitment was rewarded with an increased Liberal vote, based on previous Westminster Elections.

Although he has not contested an election since that time, John remains true to Liberal principles and is still a supporter of the current Liberal Democratic Party. He certainly made campaigning an enjoyable event!

Guilden Sutton, Cheshire, England, March 1997

John Calder at Frankfurt

Maurice Girodias

It has taken me all of a dozen years to confront at last this blank page which awaits my words. It was at the Frankfurt Book Fair, on a busy day, with hundreds of publishers scurrying around in Halle 7-A, and I had just managed to buttonhole my old friend John Calder at long last. Anyone who knows John is aware of the fact that you can't get a fiver out of the man even if your life depends on it. Well, my life depended on whether I could raise five thousand dollars somehow within the next forty-eight hours – or my business would go under, once again. What a tragedy, you can't say no, please John.

"Leave me alone," John was saying. "You and your money problems, you know…Listen, not only don't I have the money, but I never *lend* money. It's a sure way to lose friends, you know that don't you? But money is easy to find here, why don't you ask the others?"

"Fat chance," I muttered somberly. John had been my last hope.

"Write your memoirs," he said. To get rid of me, quite obviously.

"Don't be an idiot, John!" I groaned. "I've got to get the money within two days maximum, otherwise it's all over. And it's only five thousand, it's really nothing, I'm sure you could - "

"Seriously," he cut me off, his pink face puckered in earnestness. "The autobiography of Maurice Girodias, that's a sure winner. Everyone will want it, the Americans especially; they're flashing their chequebooks all over the place. All you have to do is announce the project, that's all. You don't even have to write a line. Five thousand! It's chicken feed."

"You really think so? I said, somewhat flattered by the implications. That Calder was a sly one, a Scotsman with a vengeance.

"Of course! They all respect you here. They know who you are...You've been had by some, you have swindled a few others, you have made and lost fortunes. People like a scoundrel who's down on his luck; they understand and sympathise...Plus all your escapades with the ladies...and that zany nightclub of yours, La Grande Severine, hah, that's a whole story in itself! And, of course, I must admit, whether you knew what you were doing or not, you've discovered ten times more talent, as a publisher, than the three thousand noodles here. Think of it Sam Beckett. *Lolita.* Miller. Genet. *Naked Lunch. Candy. Story of O*, goddammit! And your crazy fight with Donleavy over the rights of *The Ginger Man*! And losing the rights of *Candy* to a bunch of American pirates...Well, the list is endless – Georges Bataille, Iris Owens, eh? And *Zorba the Greek*, de Sade, Alex Trocchi, Frank Harris!...You must tell me who wrote *Story of O* one of these days... And funny books like *The Sexual Life of Robinson Crusoe*. Akbar del Pimbo! It takes lots of balls to market stuff like that to porno fans and not be gunned down by one of those maniacs. They have no humour."

"Well said," I opined.

"You know what you did?" asked friend John. "You disarmed the opposition. Just like that. All those prune-faced puritans in Britain and in the States, banned in London, banned in Boston; they've been silenced by the sheer ridicule of their position, just because of what you published. Just as if the emperor had clothes on after all. Your defense of real masterpieces, *Lolita, Naked Lunch*, even *Sexus*, or the *Ginger Man,* this puts you in a class apart. No other publisher has ever done that. You are a liberator. I admire you." John's watery eyes belied his words, but, never mind, they were good words. Whatever I may have said about his tightness, he was generous when it came to fair praise.

"Well, John," I said, "that's all very kind of you but - "

"Let me finish!" John interrupted, very excited. "I know what I owe you. You practically forced me to publish *Tropic of Cancer* in England. I was terrified, but you convinced me to do it. That's really when I became a publisher. You've helped me, and you've helped dozens of those other characters around us. You changed the world, that's what you did. You made it safe for sex. You know what they call you in Tangiers? The Lenin of the Sexual Revolution. Hah! Sin-

gle-handed you did what Churchill and Roosevelt together couldn't have pulled off in a century: You destroyed Anglo-Saxon censorship, *blaam*, all by yourself."

"Oh, John," I said weakly.

"That's right, my friend. You're a personage. All those punks here are not fit to shine your boots. All right now, you just make a book out of that. It will sell like hot cakes."

"But, John, I keep telling you that it will take *time*…Perhaps you could write it for me, you seem to know the story," I suggested.

"Don't be silly, you have to do it yourself. It may take twelve years or more, if you ask me, but never mind. For now all you have to do is simply talk about it; you don't have to go to work on it. Stir them up, but be vague, tell them a few of your stories. If you're not a complete fool, you will have your money on time, five thousand dollars, and much more probably."

It was really tempting. And it sounded so simple, easy and natural, the way he was describing the move.

"Okay, how do I begin?" I asked.

"Right now you don't have to do a thing. I'll do the groundwork for you. I have one hour before my next meeting, that's ample. But you, you mustn't make a move, understand?"

"Well, all right. But may I ask what you propose to do?"

"Simple. You know the best seller mentality, eh? Well, all I have to do is to give them an image of your book as a potential best seller. You know – *By the Man Who Gave You* Lolita! Candy! Zorba the Greek! The King of Porn! That's the pitch. Easy. You know what maniacs they are with their million dollar deals, bidding and outbidding one another to get the winner…a book nobody has the time to read or even write…a name, a vague idea… and who cares if in the end it falls flat on its face, because by the time it comes out they forgot how much they paid for it in the first place…Ah yes, success, best sellers, miracles, millions of dollars, big reviews, that's the name of the game, that's why we're all in it, little boy gamblers, all of us…Yes, yes…So you see how simple it is, all I have to do is drop on a few of them, the true believers, and ask them to lend me five thousand dollars. And just as I did when you asked me for the money, they will say to me: Why do you need it, John? And I will answer: 'I just convinced Girodias he should write his autobiography, and I want to secure the British rights on the spot. He's broke, as usual, five thousand will do it, etc., etc.' You'll have your cheque within twenty-four hours, guaranteed."

"Johnny my boy, you're amazing! I do wonder why Her Majesty the Queen did not single you out, a man like you could have saved the empire."

"Oh, forget it, will you? What you have to do is simply to go to the Frankfurter Hof, sit in the bar, and look mysterious. But not a word to anyone about the book, eh?"

"I shall obey joyfully. God bless you, my precious friend." And I watched him fondly as he trotted off on his little Teddy bear legs into the gesticulating, negotiating populace.

It would be pointless to document the sordid details; suffice it to say that I was soon deluged with contracts, plus a pocketful of some fifteen thousand in cash, which I fingered voluptuously through the tweed, feeling rather as if I had discovered a bundle of bank notes wrapped in old newspaper, abandoned by some absentminded bur-glar under a bench.

That money came to me in a dream. When I woke up, the money was gone and I still had to write the book. I did a few pages, at least to give myself a clear conscience. I tore them up. I tried again. Worse still. That damned first page...As we all know, the first page is the hardest one; that's where most people fail.

My story is not easy to write. It took me all those years and many tribulations to get close to it at last. Hard years, stark and punishing years; my life was turning against me for having treated it so badly. And in the end that's what saved me. I lost everything and finally accepted my loss. Then I could start reconstructing myself. And write that first page! It may not be brilliant, but it has cost me a lot. And now I have a past and a future again, and between the two a fulcrum – this book.

*From **The Frog Prince**, Crown Publishing, New York*

"It seems I have known John Calder all my life..."

Jim Haynes

It seems I have known John Calder all my life. We have been friends since 1959. Therefore, it's true to say I have known him all my adult life. (I was born in Louisiana, lived in Venezuela in my teens, and journeyed to Scotland in my early 20s – thanks to Uncle Sam and the United States Air Force.)

In the spring of 1959, after serving almost three years in the Air Force listening nightly to the Russian Air Defense Command, I managed to obtain permission from both the American and British governments to be "de-mobbed" in Scotland. The pretense involved wanting to continue my studies at the University of Edinburgh, but in fact I wished to continue my love affair with the city of Edinburgh. (An affair, I might add, that continues some 40 years later with just as much intensity.) But suddenly without the monthly paycheque (and with no financial support from my family) it immediately became imperative that I had to find a way to keep myself alive.

To make a very long story short, in the autumn of 1959, I opened what was reputedly the first all paperback bookstore in Great Britain appropriately called "The Paperback". And it is here where John and I first meet and develop our on-going friendship. Located between the Old Quad and the new George Square Expansion, the bookshop was in a perfect location, an oasis, a "watering hole" as many stopped to have a cup of tea or coffee once or twice a day.

One of my first actions was a series of letters to publishers to announce the shop's opening, to ask for a catalogue of their paper-

Edinburgh International Festival 1962

"*The Novel Today*"

Programme & Notes

International Writers' Conference

20th - 24th August
McEwan Hall Edinburgh

PRICE FIVE SHILLINGS

" People jumping up to confess they were homosexuals or heterosexuals; a Registered Heroin Addict leading the young Scottish opposition to the literary tyranny of the Communist Hugh MacDiarmid... an English woman novelist describing her communications with her dead daughter; a Dutch homosexual, former male nurse, now a Catholic convert, seeking someone to baptize him; a bearded Sikh with hair down to his waist declaring on the platform that homosexuals were incapable of love, just as (he said) hermaphrodites were incapable of orgasm (Stephen Spender, in the chair, murmured that he should have thought they could have two)... "

– *Quotation from a letter Mary McCarthy wrote to Hannah Arendt describing the Conference*

backs and to seek a credit arrangement. Soon thereafter, John Calder himself arrived on my doorstep, order book in hand. He got the first of many large orders and I got my credit arrangement. Shortly afterwards several large boxes of paperbacks arrived from John's warehouse. These books were displayed, recommended and sold. Further orders ensued. John has said many times that The Paperback was one of his most important outlets. We certainly sold a lot of Calderbooks. There were many reasons for this: 1. The books themselves. 2. The bookshop attracted the kind of people that would be attracted to the kind of literature John published. And 3. I promoted, recommended, displayed and pushed Calderbooks at every opportunity.

During the 1960 Frankfurt Book Fair, John and I spent a great deal of time together – as we were to do over some 25 future book messes. When John would have an appointment away from his Stand, I usually managed to look after things until his return.

In the autumn of 1961, John organized a literary tour of Great Britain in order to introduce and publicize three of his authors to the British book-buying public. Marguerite Duras, Nathalie Sarraute, and Alain Robbe-Grillet were not exactly household names at the time. But John was determined that their books would receive a critical appreciation in Britain. And I was roped-in to help co-ordinate the Edinburgh end of the tour. The success of this venture led to a decision to ask Lord Harewood, the then Director of the Edinburgh International Festival, to add a literary element to the festival. We asked Lord Harewood to allow us to organize a Writers' Conference as part of the official festival in 1962. And to our amazement, Lord Harewood bought the idea. With his blessing, (and with added input from George Orwell's widow, Sonia Orwell), we found ourselves organizing what many people later believed as one of the best parties of the decade. We had a green light to invite anyone we wished. John and Sonia handled the invitations. John lobbied the British Council, the cultural Attaches, the publishers and anyone else who might "sponsor" (i.e. pay for) a writer to attend our event. I would co-ordinate the Edinburgh end and arrange the hospitality and parties. In order to hold down costs, it was decided we would farm out our distinguished authors to appropriate Edinburgh hosts. My Frederick Street flat became our conference office with John and Sonia arriving and departing at regular intervals. The telephone line was constantly busy with me seeking information on the latest addition to the list and John and

Sonia wanting to know where this or that writer would be staying. (No faxes or e-mail in those days.)

Approximately 70 novelists from all corners of the world participated in a gigantic free-for-all dialogue with each other and with a large audience of several thousand enthusiastic individuals. This took place every afternoon in a giant barrel of a McEwan Hall – located some fifty metres from The Paperback Bookshop. The "star" for me was Henry Miller. But there was someone there to suit everyone's taste: Mary McCarthy, Niccolo Tucci, Norman Mailer, Lawrence Durrell, Colin MacInnes, Angus Wilson, William Burroughs, Alex Trocchi, Kushwang Singh, Hugh MacDiarmid, Harry Mulish, Cees Nooteboom, Aleksandar Stefanovic.

The audience was encouraged to participate, but they needed very little encouragement. It was a literary circus, a zoo, a madhouse. It was fantastic. The audience loved it. The press loved it. The delegates loved it. And John, Sonia and I had a ball! (Even Lord Harewood was pleased.) The afternoon party atmosphere continued into the evening in various restaurants and at parties all over Edinburgh's New Town. Of course there was gossip and scandal. Norman Mailer was involved in an argument with the distinguished Oxford don (and translator of *Dr. Zhivago*), Max Hayward, that almost got out of hand. John asked me to deliver a message to the leader of the Yugoslav delegation. Somehow or other, I failed to get this to him. He became so upset that it required major diplomatic maneuvering from John and others to prevent him from taking the entire Yugoslav contribution out of the festival. This almost caused a major scandal.

I think the following quotation from a letter Mary McCarthy wrote to Hannah Arendt will demonstrate how one of the writers felt about the week's event: "Tucci turned up in Edinburgh, where I went to a Conference on the Novel in the middle of August – a fantastic affair; did you read anything about it?...Aside from him the Conference was bizarre enough. People jumping up to confess they were homosexuals or heterosexuals; a Registered Heroin Addict leading the young Scottish opposition to the literary tyranny of the Communist Hugh MacDiarmid (who had rejoined the party, after being out of it for years following the Hungarian Revolution); the Yugoslav group in schism and their ambassador threatening to pull the Belgrade Opera and Ballet out of the Festival because the non-official delegate had been allowed to speak before the official delegate; an English woman novelist describing her communications with her dead daughter; a Dutch homosexual, former male nurse, now a Catholic convert, seeking someone to baptize him; a bearded Sikh with hair down to his waist declaring on the platform that homosexuals were incapable of love, just as (he said) hermaphrodites were incapable of orgasm (Stephen Spender, in the chair, murmured that he should have thought they could have two). And all of this before an audience of over two thousand people per day, mostly, I suppose, Scottish Presbyterians. The most striking fact was the number of lunatics both on the platform and in the public. One young woman novelist was released temporarily from a mental hospital in order to attend the Conference, and she was one of the milder cases. I confess I enjoyed it enormously. Do you know an Austrian writer called Erich Fried? He and I made common cause in trying to establish a plane of sanity between the lunatics and philistines, though we were at odds ourselves on the validity of psychoanalysis (his madness or my philistinism)....(from *Between Friends – The Correspondence of Hannah Arendt and Mary McCarthy 1949 – 1975*, Edited with an introduction by Carol Brightman, published by Harcourt Brace & Company; this letter written from Paris on the 28th of September 1962*)*

I know that John and I and many others had a great time. Friendships were born that continue to blossom to this day. No matter how one measures it, the Writers' Conference was a major success. So much so that Lord Harewood backed our proposal to allow John and his team to organize a Drama Conference for the 1963 Edinburgh Festival.

This time Kenneth Tynan would serve as Chairman (and Sonia Orwell's replacement) and would assist with the invitations and with the conference itself. The success and the reputation of the Writers' Conference made it much easier to get guests. Over 120 delegates accepted the invitation to attend. Once again The Paperback provided an exhibition of books by all the delegates attending. They were displayed and sold in the McEwan Hall as well as The Paperback.

Again the conference attracted an excited audience who packed the McEwan Hall every afternoon for six days. This public attempted "to get in on the act" as much as Kenneth Tynan, the conference chairman, would allow. Once again the conference was a world's Who's Who of dramatists and theatre personalities.

But let me backtrack. The success of producing intimate dramatic

DAVID APPLEFIELD

66 We have gone through the wars together and this shared experience produces a warm fusion of kindred spirit, of mutual admiration and respect. **99**

- Jim Haynes

readings in my bookshop in 1960 led to the creation of a larger space, "The Howff". We opened just before the 1961 festival and had a big success during the festival. But problems with my partner ensued. This led to my seeking (and finding) the premises in St. James's Court, just off the Lawnmarket. Without going into the complicated evolution of the Traverse Theatre Club, let me just say that John was a major source of energy and inspiration. His advice and support was invaluable.

About this time, John inherited Ledlanet, a large estate in Kinross-shire, about an hour and a half from Edinburgh. This meant John would spend more and more time in Scotland in the years that followed. And my flat in Frederick Street and later in Great King Street always had a bed for John.

Today as most of you know, John has a home in France, in Montreuil, just one minute from Paris. I have lived the past 27 years in Paris, teaching Media Studies at the University of Paris. We have a love for Paris and *la vie Parisienne*. We manage to see each other often and to plan future schemes, to talk about old friends and old projects, and to contemplate it all. The two of us are complete opposites in many ways. But we have gone through the wars together and this shared experience produces a warm fusion, of kindred spirit, of mutual admiration and respect. It's been almost forty years since John walked into my life. I hope we have another forty more together. Together – and separately – we have made the world around us jump a bit...

JOHN MINIHAN

JOHN & DAVID

John Calder and David Applefield

Sacred John

David Applefield

I met John Calder today for lunch. A favourite place of his called Le Franklin in Montreuil, the core of the *Banlieue Rouge* on the eastern edge of Paris, a town that John once coined the Montparnasse of the *fin de siecle*. And before his stylish plate of tomato and mozzarella arrived he was telling me about the Christianization of Rome. Somehow the conversation slipped into Henry Miller and that afternoon in the mid-sixties when John led his famed author around London. As we drained our first *pichet* of Cote de Rhone I learned how Maimonides put bread on his table and why the price of books needed to be fixed to combat the deadening commercial trend that threatens the intellectual and cultural life in the world.

He's written another two obituaries this week, more fallen friends in the world of literature and art. John has written over a thousand obituaries and it has taken me a number of years to understand just how apt this hybrid form of writing is to its maker. In a day and a thousand words John Calder captures his subject's quintessential contribution to mankind. He coins lasting terms in which the world of daily things and people remember a single artist, and with the elegance that often accompanies irony he supplements his own living with their death. The food chain of cultural transgression is served. For John the most frightening truth is the thought that one's existence may be forgotten, the psychic plumb line he shared with Samuel Beckett, by far his most significant author, and the man who has probably impressed him most in this world.

The *plat du jour* is *couscous* with *brochette du mouton*, but John takes the trout. He has become very anti-meat these last years, distrustful of all governments' treatment of public heath issues, and attracted by the lightness of eating. John Calder is happy with a raw carrot, a bunch of grapes, a pile of radishes and a glass or two of Sancerre as fuel. Knowing John is like befriending Estragon in person. The Beckettian character suggests: "Why don't we hang ourselves?" He'd never do it, although there is always a somber, available necktie fastened neatly around his neck and the idea doesn't terrify the man. In terms of terror, spiders however are more effective and John's true cowardice comes forward in blushing colours. And when it comes to sublime angst, just mention eggs. Eggs, in any shape or form, sends this Scottish-Canadian publisher into fits of terror that only Freud himself could understand.

Sacred John.

Our friendship began as many do, I had a manuscript, he had a publishing house. We met at the Frankfurt Book Fair, an event that once had great importance for him and now he no longer frequents. Today, most professional encounters are with authors whose manuscripts he's not returned or whose books need reprinting or worse, creditors who want to skin him alive. He actually saves money each year by staying away. For John, debt is no shame, it's almost an emblem for publishing serious work. Concerning budget, John Calder's operation runs like the economy of a third world country. The interest alone is crippling. But life goes on, books keep coming out, and authors and titles which the world of big business has little time for – survive. John claims to have published over 6000 titles, over 20 Nobel Prize winners, and keeps over a million books in print spread over three continents. At 72 at least half of his time is spent driving from bookshop to bookshop and educating buyers as to what they need and what they've sold since his last visit, which was sometimes as many as three years earlier. John doesn't really *sell* his books, he *teaches* them in the minutes he has to make his sales pitch. His catalogue is his curriculum; his authors his soul mates (even the difficult ones), his titles his life. Younger booksellers these days don't know what to make of him. Many have no choice other than to order more books. Lots, of course, get returned, (the publisher's nemesis) but many stick. He once told me that every copy of every book he sells, he thinks of as a major triumph. No wonder why poets love him.

He orders another *pichet* of *rouge*, cheese is coming. Form and the habit of good old days prevents John from ever letting the wine dry up.

After Frankfurt nearly 20 years ago he suggested a rendez-vous at the Hotel Odeon-Michelet, where Genet lived, in the publishers' district of Paris opposite the Theatre de l'Odeon where he'd spend the nights he'd not be at one of Paris' three opera houses. He flipped through my stack of manuscript pages and promised an answer in three weeks. (Three years later he confessed that if he still hadn't answered yet that it was a good sign.) It *was* a good sign, and I decided to publish him first. I published in the journal I edit, *Frank*, the first excerpt from his lengthy opus magnus *In Defense of Literature*, the work that lends its name to this Festschrift. Later I published several of his poems including one called *Gourmandise* in which he names Paris as the city he's chosen to die in as he swallows oysters and feels guilty for such indulgence in a world that knows great fathoms of pain and strife.

John has been attacked for a great many things, his organizational skills, unpaid bills, unrealistic expectations, political leftism, publishing immoral texts, battling unpopular ideas, embodying a strange shyness...but at the end of the day these ultimately dissolve into the trivial or pedestrian. The lasting quality is that John Calder is a kind human being. I've rarely met anyone with more compassion or empathy for people in pain than him. Admittedly, much has changed in the world of publishing over the half century John Calder has participated in the industry. Commerce, marketing, design, distribution, rights, production, shipping, literary tastes have all gone through radical transformations, but one thing remains constant: books are about ideas and the sharing of those ideas through the medium of printed language. And John Calder whose Ludite tendencies help characterize him falsely as a dinosaur at the millenium's end – (okay he still calls the Internet, the Interweb) – as publisher, editor, friend of authors and cultural guerrilla has never lost that primal consciousness of what a good book is.

We order two espressos and I can see that John is happy with the moment. He's unhurried. He's reflecting. The sun is shining. And he is in France where the literary life is still revered. The sun is shining through the glass door of the restaurant and John reaches down to pet the funny head of the resident German shepherd. "Maybe I should just stop, stay here and write my memoirs…"

There's a silence.

Tomorrow at the crack of dawn he'll be on the EuroStar tunneling back to his tiny London office, then it will be a mad dash for Birmingham, Sheffield, Leeds, Oxford and anywhere else that his hieroglyphic-coded agenda tells him he has booked himself to be. There are novels and plays to be sold and there is no such thing as stopping. The following week it is Ireland, then back to Paris, two weekends on the east coast of the United States, back to Paris, an opera in Munich, a conference in Normandy, lunch at le Franklin…

The bill comes and he lunges.

Poems for John Calder

Sorel Etrog

Soothe-case

The floor
        a white page
from wall to wall
        folded words
Lying on the floor, faces
folded faces, in
folded pages

ceiling, walls, floor
folded like a suitcase
inside folded darkness

a split in this folded cave
Air! An horizon, and
the pressing words, unfold
horizon after horizon

Sisyphus

You crack rocks with words
You use the mind as a com-
pressor
Your tongue as a chisel.

Thoughts run through your
veins
Till you are numb.

If your name was Sisyphus
You could start over again.

Montreuil

The roof
    a book cover

The walls
    peeling
    revealing

Many skins many hymns.

A Chessboard Made of Titles

You know
what they want.

Smoke rings rise around their
heads
halos of fame

You made them angels
knights and bishops
on a chessboard
made of titles

You let them play their games
the madman's game, the end
game
to seek out a revelation
sufficient in itself.

John Calder by Sorel Etrog

section four

section
four

IV

N E W   B O O K S
A N D   R E P R I N T S
1 9 9 2 & 1 9 9 3

CALDER
PUBLICATIONS

RIVERRUN
PRESS

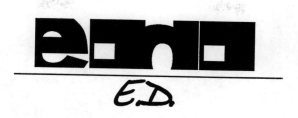

E.D.

John Calder lives 50 meters from me in Montreuil, in Colonel Delorme Street. John Calder called me for the third time (by phone), on the 3rd of January, at 7 p.m. John Calder suggested we eat together at a restaurant nearby. I said: Yes, I thanked.

John Calder took me to the Chinese restaurant, en face du Marche (he said it's the best one in Montreuil), "Imperial".

John Calder started the conversation by talking about his leftist orientation. I asked if he is a communist. John Calder said: Not exactly, but…pretty.

John Calder was in schools all over the world: Ecosse, Angleterre, Canada, Autriche (we were speaking in French, with English and Slav accents.) John Calder got married in 1949. John Calder had a daughter: Janine. John Calder separated from his wife in 1959. John Calder said he thinks his wife is dead (I repeated: think!?). John Calder said he doesn't know. You can find out, I said. John Calder said: No. John Calder said he believes his daughter is dead too. I asked: Why do you think that? John Calder said: No word from them for such a long time that they must be dead. Why do you think they are dead if there is no word, I asked. John Calder said: They must be dead. I said: You are a monster Mr. Calder (as soon as I said that I didn't think it any more) I laughed. John Calder laughed too.

John Calder is an actor. John Calder will appear in a play (I forgot: Beckett or Ionesco) in Paris, next month.

John Calder founded his publishing house in 1949. John Calder forgot which was the first book he published. John Calder has published more than 6000 titles.

John Calder remarried in 1960 a woman from Dugi Otok. John Calder had a daughter, Anastasia. John Calder got divorced. John Calder is not in touch with his ex-wife. John Calder is not in touch

66 John Calder says he is doing what
has to be done. 99

– E.D.

with his daughter. John Calder is not in touch with his grandchildren. John Calder and I started with wine. We finished with sake. John Calder suggested a glass of whisky at his house. I agreed. John Calder's place is a true pigsty. Comfortable. Books and papers everywhere. John Calder writes obituaries about people who are still alive. John Calder showed me some of his published obituaries. I asked: How much does it pay. John Calder said: Pretty well. I asked: How much did you get for this one (Marguerite Duras)? John Calder said the price.

John Calder chooses about 30 names every month, and submits the list. The editor chooses 12 to 15 (I wonder if it is good luck or bad luck to not be chosen?)

John Calder has written about 2,000 obituaries up to now. I asked: How many of them are still alive? John Calder said: About one third. I didn't know what to do with the thought: Is the name John Calder on somebody else's list? Instead I asked: Would you write an obituary for me? He didn't answer. I mentioned my ephemeral projects for here and now. John Calder didn't say anything.

After a silence he said: I am doing a positive thing. I said: Yes.

He picked up his whisky glass. I picked up mine. We toasted. I asked with how many women he had made love. John Calder said he never really calculated. John Calder said there was a period when he could not sleep, and then he was counting. He came to the approximate number of more than 300. I shared my shame, mentioning my modest experience of making love, compared to the number he mentioned. John Calder said he used to make love to a woman who had extremely right wing views. I asked: How could you? John Calder said that it worked pretty well, but he discovered he couldn't discuss politics with her. John Calder said he was never attracted to rich women. He was always attracted to poor women. (I asked what are the criteria for rich and poor?) John Calder said poor means normal. John Calder said he feels responsible for the suicide of one woman. (I said every one is responsible for his own choice.)

John Calder said he is thinking about the suicide "à la Seneca." Seneca cut his veins in warm water and passed his last hours talking with his friends.

John Calder went to the opera 80 times, in 1996. John Calder has attended 2,822 opera performances in his life (up to the 3rd of January 1997) (783 different operas).

John Calder is in a lawsuit against the States. He is fighting for price control on books. John Calder has an office in London. John Calder has an 80 year old employee there, who wished to stay on instead of retire. John Calder has an office in New York. John Calder travels all the time. John Calder has an office in New York. John Calder travels all the time. John Calder says he is doing what has to be done.

John Calder said: Life is suffering.

John Calder said: Everything will be forgotten.

John Calder said: I will buy an apartment near the Croix de Chavaux in Montreuil.

John Calder said he would put his huge library there (which is now in boxes in his garage).

I asked to whom will he leave his library? John Calder said: I have nobody.

John Calder was born on the 25th of January 1927. John Calder said he will be 70 this month. John Calder said: I don't know after.

I said: After you will be 71.

It was 3 o'clock in the morning.

I got drunk with John Calder.

Montreuil, 4th of January 1997
E.D. (I'm a normal woman who admires John Calder)

André Derval

Care About Literature anD thE aRts

John Calder fait partie de ce clan rare d'hommes ayant marqué l'histoire de l'édition au vingtième siècle. Son intelligence et la sûreté de son goût, tant pour le texte publié que pour sa présentation, lui ont permis de constituer, par ses forces propres, un catalogue d'oeuvres littéraires que des maisons d'édition bien plus puissantes n'ont pu égaler. Je ne reviendrai pas sur le déroulement chronologique de sa carrière – je crois qu'elle est traitée dans une section de ce dossier d'hommage – mais je voudrais ici donner quelques éléments, quelques points saillants de son entreprise. Et auparavant rapporter les circonstances de ma rencontre avec lui et les termes de notre fréquentation.

Grâce à l'intermédiaire d'Olivier Corpet, Directeur de l'Institut Mémoires de l'édition contemporaine, où j'occupe les fonctions de responsable des fonds d'éditeurs et de quelques fonds d'auteurs, dont Louis-Ferdinand Céline et Samuel Beckett (publiés tous deux chez Calder), j'ai fait la connaissance de John Calder en 1994, alors qu'il venait de décider de s'installer en banlieue parisienne afin de poursuivre au mieux ses activités, en butte aux tracasseries thatcheriennes qui frappaient le domaine culturel indépendant. D'emblée mon attention fut retenue par l'abord extrêmement modeste du personnage, ayant à son actif une expérience professionnelle et intellectuelle des plus remarquables mais qui n'en faisait pas étalage; cette exceptionnelle bonhomie (d'autant plus exceptionnelle en France, où le moindre plumitif se rengorge d'importance) s'accompagnait d'une grande cocasserie dans l'expression (de mère québecoise, il parle un français irréprochable), notamment durant l'évocation de ses souvenirs. Dans le même temps, je remarquai son impérieux souci de clarté pour l'interlocuteur – au travers d'une foule de projets jaillissant dans le cours de la conversation – et j'ai gardé de cette première entrevue l'image de quelqu'un hors du commun, mu par une profonde vitalité, guidé par la conviction de l'unité de sa démarche.

Par la suite, j'ai en maintes fois l'occasion de vérifier cette première impression; je fus en charge du transfert de ses archives au moment de son déménagement de la Fonderie, à Montreuil, et depuis lors nous avons effectué de nombreux allers et retours vers la réserve de l'IMEC, où il m'apporte une aide indispensable à classer et inventorier ses papiers. Plus d'une fois également, nous avons fait en sorte de partager un repas ou verre, John Calder est toujours d'excellent conseil et je n'hésite pas à lui soumettre mes travaux. Au fil du temps, nos relations sont ainsi passées du franchement cordial à l'amical, et bien que nous accusions une différence d'âge d'environ trente ans, j'avoue ne pas n'étonner outre mesure de cette affinité, tout en demandant au lecteur d'excuser le côté présomptueux de cette dernière affirmation. Mais il est de fait qu'aucun autre éditeur de son envergure n'est capable de vous parler tout à la fois du rôle dissolvant de la censure, de l'étranglement de la création contemporaine par les nouvelles structures commerciales du livre – à savoir les concentrations de librairies et d'éditeurs – du désintérêt du pouvoir politique, mais aussi des satisfactions procurées par le "long-selling," lorsque la reconnaissance d'un auteur intervient après de longues années de vaches maigres...

On sait combien la littérature française contemporaine est redevable à John Calder, pour la diffusion de celle-ci en pays anglophones. On sait problement moins les liens personnels qu'il a su tisser avec la plupart de ses auteurs français. La bibliothèque de l'Université Bloomington partage avec l'IMEC le privilège d'abriter la correspondance qu'il a entretenue avec ceux-ci; ayant été en mesure de comparer ces lettres avec celles d'autres éditeurs, ie m'est pour le moins évident qu'elles figurent parmi les plus passionnantes.

Un point particulièrement révélateur de l'originalité – et de l'importance – de la production éditoriale de John Calder se situe à mon avis dans le soin avec lequel il a mis en place l'organisation du "Theatre of Literature," autour de l'oeuvre de quelques auteurs (Samuel Beckett, Claude Simon, Wyndham Lewis), de quelques thèmes (Nouveau Roman, Cornucopia, "Anthology from Shakespeare to Beckett," Damned Publishing (40 year history of Calder Publishing...) et du concept de "Literary Triplets" (imagine-t-on le télescopage de Céline, d'Ionesco et de Lewis?), les textes concernés étant en vente à la sortie de la représentation. Selon moi, c'est dans le cadre du "Theatre of Literature" que John Calder a livré le fond de son ambition d'éditeur: être au service de l'aventure littéraire. Comme le résumait au mieux la présentation de son catalogue: "These are books for real people who care about literature and the arts, the greatest solace in troubled times. They will be your good friends."

Sunday Mirror

5d. September 8, 1963 No. 23

UPROAR AS GIRL STRIPS AT BIG CONFERENCE

By STANLEY SHIVAS

THE Queen's cousin, the 40-year-old Earl of Harewood, yesterday watched a shapely 19-year-old blonde strip and parade in the nude.

The shock strip came during the closing moments of the big Edinburgh Festival Drama Conference.

On the conference platform theatre personalities were debating "The Theatre of the Future." Heckling started as talk became more solemn. It grew into uproar.

Then art college model Anna Kesselaar, up in the balcony, dropped her bombshell —and her clothes. And the uproar became a storm.

Smiling, she began to strip at speed. Before attendants in Edinburgh's McEwan Hall could get to her she was naked.

She paraded across the balcony until she was bundled into a red plastic raincoat and hustled out of the hall.

Some of the international audience sat in shocked silence. Others cheered and clapped.

Smiled

Lord Harewood, artistic director of the Edinburgh Festival, who was the main guest, smiled faintly. Then his smile became a broad grin as he said:

"I wasn't in the least annoyed. It was a rather amusing experiment."

He went on: "One might safely say that the conference was extremely undull today."

But actor DUNCAN MACRAE said later:

"If these people wanted to raise a sensation they would have been better advised to have gone to the Rangers-Celtic football match to throw bottles at the referee. I did not appreciate the scene."

And ANNA? She said: "A lot of people were des-

Lord Harewood

An amusing experiment, says Lord Harewood

Anna Kesselaar

A giggle, says Anna

appointed by the pompous tone of the conference.

"It had achieved nothing. I and my friends, who were heckling, thought the whole thing should be jazzed up into life."

Will she get into trouble at home?

"I don't know what on earth my father will think," she said. "He had no idea what I was going to do."

Earlier the thousands of people at the conference were startled when Irish director JAMES FITZGERALD shouted at Joan Littlewood, the producer: "A lot of bloody nonsense!"

Bagpipes

JOAN LITTLEWOOD, of Theatre Workshop fame, had just declared, "We are coming to the time when every man and woman will be a genius."

Then film star CARROLL (Baby Doll) BAKER wiggled on to the platform during a discussion wearing a very tight gold lamé dress.

And someone began to play the bagpipes.

LAST WORD from Anna: "It was all a bit of a giggle."

Balcony scene—naked among the spotlamps is Anna Kesselaar. "What will father think?" she asked

104

Leonard Fenton

I had the great good fortune to meet John Calder in 1964, when I went to work at the Traverse Theatre in Edinburgh, which had acquired a lively international reputation under the chairmanship of Jim Haynes. In addition to his work as an active committee member, John was organizing literature and opera festivals – all this while running his publishing business.

The combination of his publishing and his work in the theatre led him to arrange a selection of Samuel Beckett's plays and prose to form a powerful statement and this was performed at the Edinburgh Festival of 1964 by the director Michael Geliot and myself.

This event later crystallized into what John later dubbed "The Theatre of Literature," a practical idea, which has enabled him to attract to literature some of the money from private and public sources available to theatre groups. I'm glad to say this particular hands-on activity has continued to this day and will no doubt be shortly carried to the European Continent.

Recent work with John has enabled me to watch him teaching at an international school in Paris (he also taught at a French university) and I envied those fascinated teenage students, who benefited from his wide knowledge of literature, history and the arts.

And we have witnessed his fighting spirit as a publisher – the court battles defending his publishing against out-dated obscenity laws – his work for the net book agreement, to say nothing of his battles to get the British Government to support the Arts. The latter battle will lead to a National Arts Rally in Hyde Park, London on May 1st and 2nd, 1999.

It would be good to meet there and wish John Calder, Publisher, a Happy Birthday.

“ I was astonished when I learned that John was keeping a tally of his attendance at opera performances. I wonder how many performances he averages in a year... ”

— *Lila Fenwick*

LILA FENWICK

Lila Fenwick

When I agreed to participate in this project, I wanted to recount some amusing or interesting encounters with John. I considered him a friend but I could not forget that I was his lawyer. There is almost nothing I can write which might not violate the rule of confidentiality governing the attorney/client relationship. I am, accordingly, limiting myself to general and unsubstantiated impressions of my 'client'.

John, obviously has always felt free to ignore the cognoscenti. Recently, he has obviously been disregarding arguments - that book publishing is not merely endangered, but passé. A number of years ago, when I was representing him, he certainly did not slavishly follow my legal or other opinions. I, along with the rest of his circle, have learned to accept his independent cast of mind.

I met John in the late 1970s, when he was establishing a beachhead here in New York for his British publishing company. He had several projects, legal and financial, and I was consulted on some of them.

Although I have not seen John for a number of years, my impressions of him remain vivid. He had charm and fierceness in his determination to publish serious literature. I recall his saying that he not only likes to publish books and to read them, but to see books and to feel them.

John was always a delight for a lawyer, because he projected a sense of optimism. Lawyers are usually dealing with the "worst case scenario." In John's case, there were plans for expanding, re-configuring, re-capitalizing, etc. his operations. His business proposals might be considered risky for the cautious, but they invariably had merit. John was constantly casting about for ways not to survive but to succeed – and to succeed spectacularly. At the same time, he was always very serious about the process of publishing and the quality of his product.

I can imagine an autobiography of John filled with heroic tales of how perils were met and obstacles were overcome. A description of John's life, along those lines, would be true, but it would hardly be complete. John, while not a Sybarite, was also committed to having fun. He enjoyed the so-called 'good things' – food, drink, music, dancing. He always seemed buoyant and good humoured, even when facing difficulties.

He was dedicated to the arts. In the 1990s, his interests are deemed elitist. I don't think he would object to that characterization. He has turned his avocations into his vocation. I assume his interest in opera fuelled his publication of the English National Opera librettos. The usual libretto contains only text of the opera in one or two languages. John's libretti were models of scholarship, containing historical information supplemented by musical annotation.

John discovered that I liked opera. I discovered that John loved it! I was astonished when I learned that John was keeping a tally of his attendance at opera performances. I wonder how many performances he averages in a year.

His taste in opera diverged from mine. John was more venturesome. He liked the obscure, the modern, the newly discovered. In the past few years I have become more interested in the new. Can it be John's influence?

Over lunch one day, during a discussion about the Berlioz opera "Les Troyens", I expressed my reservations about the behaviour of Aneas. Although this conversation took place fifteen or more years ago, John's response has resonated with me. With a wink and a chuckle, he replied: "Oh, Lila, Aneas was merely following his destiny." Like Aneas, John internalized his destiny. In John's case it was a mission to publish books.

Well after fifty years, John deserves bravos and hurrahs. To paraphrase the title of that old American movie: "It has been a wonderful life."

John Fletcher

A Festschrift is an occasion for taking stock, chiefly of the achievement of the recipient being honoured, of course, but not exclusively; to those paying their respects, it also offers the opportunity to reflect on their own itinerary, especially where it intersects with that of the honoured.

In the case of John Calder and myself, our paths first crossed when I was compiling a bibliography of the works of Samuel Beckett in the 1960s; the relationship deepened when I became one of his authors in the 1970s, and reached its apogee when he entrusted me with the translation of Claude Simon's masterpiece *The Georgics*, which occupied me on and off for most of the 1980s. Though not nearly as impressive as his fifty years of publishing, my writing career has been quite a lengthy one, as I realised when emptying the file cabinets in my university office following my recent retirement. I came across a folder whose existence I had all but forgotten about, and when I discovered that it contained an unpublished translation of mine- of a poem by Samuel Beckett, made at the author's request – it seemed appropriate to offer this to John Calder *en homage*, since it is probably as Beckett's English publisher that John will best be remembered in the future.

The file was marked "Beginning to End", this, as Jack MacGowran's friends will recall, was the title of a programme of extracts from the works of Samuel Beckett which the actor compiled with the author's assistance for Irish television in the mid 1960s. It was, if I remember rightly, one of the first of several such anthologies: the formula soon proved popular with performers and public alike. The people in charge of television in Dublin were so pleased with the programme that they submitted it for the Italia Prize, the rules of which stipulated that scripts had to be translated into French. MacGowran asked Beckett to do it, but being otherwise engaged Sam requested that I undertake

DAVID APPLEFIELD

JOHN & SAM

John Calder never had his photograph
taken with Samuel Beckett.

the version. I translated large chunks of *From an Abandoned Work* and *Watt*, neither of which had at the time been rendered into French, as well as the title poem from the 1935 collection *Echo's Bones*. So far as I am aware, that particular poem still has not been translated to this day. I found my version in the folder marked "Beginning to End", thick with the dust of over thirty years storage. I had quite forgotten having made the translation. It was therefore a moving experience to rediscover it. It brought back, like Marcel's madeleine dipped in tea, the perfume of a past time when I was corresponding frequently with John Calder about Beckett's works (and about my own book, *New Directions in Literature*, which he accepted with flattering enthusiasm and published in 1968). So, to celebrate in a modest way the immense contribution John has made to bringing innovative literature before the English-speaking public, here is my long-lost translation, preceded by Beckett's haunting original:

asile sous mes pas tout au long de cette journee
leurs ebats assourdis quand tombe la chair
lachant sans peur et sans indulgence un vent
du sens et du non-sens passer tel l'antilope par les baguettes
pris par les asticots pour ce qu'ils sont

1935

asylum under my tread all this day
their muffled revel as the flesh falls
breaking without fear of favour wind
the gantelope of sense and nonsense run
taken by the maggots for what they are

1966, revised 1998

J/AM

Laurence Durrell, Esq.,
c/o P. F. du Sautoy, Esq.,   31st December, 1962.
Messrs. Faber & Faber Ltd.,
24, Russell Square,
LONDON. W.C.1.

Dear Mr. Durrell,

   I am writing, very belatedly, to thank you for
coming to Edinburgh and for your great help in making the
first Writers' Conference go. I hope you enjoyed yourself,
Henry Miller certainly seems to have.

   Can you tell me if we owe you money? The accounts
are in a terrible tangle, as Sonia went off to France
immediately after the last day, and Jim Haynes was also away.
Now it is very difficult to get people to remember just who
had tickets, who was paid their fare etc. I have a feeling
that we owe you for your fare to Edinburgh and that you have
been too polite to remind us up to now. Could you please
let me know.

   I am trying to plan something else for next year and
will write you about this shortly.

   All best wishes for the New Year.

        Yours sincerely,

        John Calder.

Mary Folliet

John Calder and I met because of another great man of letters – Samuel Beckett.

On Boxing Day 1989, in the company of hundreds of shivering tweedy academics, I took a frigid Amtrak train whose heating system was out of order from New York to Washington D.C., for the annual MLA convention. Upon arrival, I learned that Beckett had died. Stunned and aggrieved I went to browse the booksellers' stalls, where I was drawn to a discreetly displayed Beckett tribute – a small photo with birth and death dates. There I met a compact, distinguished gentleman sporting what I came to appreciate as his signature sartorial style, a gray pin-stripe suit. Mr. Calder and I commiserated and hit it off instantly.

Since then John has become a close friend, confidant and convivial dinner companion in New York and Paris, where we indulge our taste for oysters, seafood and fine Burgundies as well as lilting craic, a fond Irish word he taught me. One of our habitual topics is music: he tells me about opera and I tell him about jazz. But perhaps more significantly he has become an eager consultant on reading lists for my literature seminars at SUNY Empire State College and an enthusiastic guest speaker when his busy international schedule permits.

No tweedy academic, John is an inspired and inspiring teacher, whether lecturing on Beckett, as he did in the summer term of 1990, or offering an arabesque on the post-World War II literary scene in my spring 1996 seminar, The Postwar Blues: Existentialism and the Beats.

Students are charmed by him as he illuminates not only the assigned texts but also the cultural milieu of their composition and confides titillating insider gossip.

His passionate devotion to this literary enterprise ("In the beginning was the Word" – John 1: I, my favorite Gospel since childhood indoctrination) is infectious; he entertains as he instructs and gracefully shares his erudition and wisdom with wit and éclat. Witnessing his classroom performance is a privileged experience for my students and me. And every conversation with John, whether over champagne at la Coupole or vodka at The Cedar Tavern, is a sparkling learning experience. Often I am compelled to take notes.

Professionally and personally I have been immeasurably enriched by the generous friendship of the impeccable man John Calder and I'm deeply grateful that destiny led me to that Amtrak igloo, that Beckett display, that great little man in the gray pinstripe suit in December 1989. My life hasn't been the same since that fateful encounter.

Merci beaucoup et Santé!

Mary Folliet
Literature and Writing Mentor
SUNY Empire State College

Lord Harewood

Before we collaborated on a couple of quite elaborate ventures at the Edinburgh Festival, I knew John Calder as a publisher who was musical and courageous as well as innovative. By that I mean that he went for what he believed in, which I thought was good, and that what he believed in was not always going to be best-selling material, for which I admired him.

As I got to know him during our preparation of the two Festival ventures - a Literary Conference and the following year a Drama Conference - I found out more about him. The most important thing was that he was a man of his word. If he said (and he did) «We shall make ends meet and the Conference won't cost the Festival a penny. » I felt confident that this would be so and it was on that basis only, that I sold the idea to the Festival Council. John is a Scot and that didn't surprise him much.

As we worked on what was a new idea for an Edinburgh Festival, something that came to surprise me was that when I asked him for the budget he was working on, he would take an envelope out of his pocket - have you noticed that people that work on the back of envelopes always have one at hand? - and improvise an answer to my question. What he wrote down involved a rough calculation of the cost of people he thought should be invited to attend (travel, hotels, fees, subsistence) which could be set against the tickets we would sell for the events. The difference between cost and box office income would be met by the profit from sale of rights - to, I came to assume (but my assumption was never confirmed), his own publishing company. The sum always seemed to come out to his (and therefore my) satisfaction, and even though, when the procedure was repeated at our next meeting, the figures were quite different, the bottom line always indicated a balance.

SHEILA COLVIN COLLECTION

John Calder, Frank Delaney and Seamus Heaney at The Edinburgh Writer's Festival, 1980

I seem to remember he used to leave the envelopes with me and I filed them under Literature or Drama Conference; an entry he seemed to find wholly natural and which I came to regard after a couple of meetings with comparable confidence. I dare say he induced trust of the same kind in his authors, which perhaps accounted for the quality of his list. It certainly made business dealings with him more of a pleasure than a chore, and I think it is quite possible that these Conferences, which added considerably to the gaiety of Festivals, didn't cost him any more than they cost the Festival Society. I hope so at least.

The point of course is that the Conferences not only came out with balanced budgets but were in themselves good.

DAVID APPLEFIELD

“Looking back on what now seem like the heady, giddy days of the late Sixties and early Seventies, we all seemed to be in the business of rebellion. I don't think that can simply be ascribed to the fact that we were all a tad younger.”

– Paul Harris

Paul Harris

L ooking back on what now seem like the heady, giddy days of the late Sixties and early Seventies, we all seemed to be in the business of rebellion. I don't think that can simply be ascribed to the fact that we were all a tad younger. I don't think that memory is unduly coloured by the passage of the years. Those were the days of a very genuine pushing back of the boundaries: not just for the sake of bloody minded youth but because there really were important things to be done and to be achieved. And I don't think it is too self indulgent to look back on that period as something of the zenith of the individual, the entrepreneur and the creative, as opposed to the destructive rebel.

In all those areas John Calder might have served as a role model. For an emerging publisher, he was probably the chap you most wanted to be. A rebel who had taken on the establishment. A publishing list of genuine stature. An intellect clearly able to identify real talent as opposed to that of transient populism.

I missed the Frankfurt Book Fair in 1970 aboard a sinking pirate radio ship in the North Sea and first met John in October 1971 at Frankfurt. In those days there were still Gentleman Publishers. They might not all have exactly been gentlemen but they were characters, in every sense of the word, utterly devoted to the call of the struggle into print. In the British section of the fair, in a vast aircraft hangar of a hall, individual publishers who were their own men – as opposed to minions of the conglomerates – like Charles Skilton, Peter Owen, Leo Cooper, Michael Balfour and John Calder. John may not exactly thank me for bracketing him with this motley crew, but all were from a mould now broken.

I vividly remember my first meeting with John that Frankfurt. It was at Charles Skilton's stand at the Fair. Against a backdrop of copies of *Fanny Hill, The Kama Sutra* and *Pussies in Boots*, Charles had

JOHN MINIHAN

Those were the days of a very genuine pushing back of the boundaries: not just for the sake of bloody minded youth but because there really were important things to be done...

— **Paul Harris**

gathered the sort of mixed bunch of multi-talented people who seemed drawn to his eclectic and frequently outrageous ambience. There was Tuppy Owens, author and creator of the *Sex Maniac's Diary* (she went on to write *Take Me I'm Yours, A Guide to Feminine Psychology* in the days long before political correctness intruded on the freedom of expression.) There was Jim Haynes, the peripatetic legend and the man who probably knows more people than anybody else on the planet. There was Leonard Houldsworth, who then worked for Charles but who went on to edit a whole stable of, er, colourful special interest magazines now accepted as almost staple fodder. The dapper Charles, as was his wont in those days, was in the company of an exotic lady of dark hue: he used to stick an ad in the Frankfurter Zeitung the week before the fair and go out a few days early to interview up to fifty girls. And then there was John Calder...

As a group of people, you could hardly imagine a more intrinsically subversive lot. If we had been meeting on the turf of The Met they would have undoubtedly have run us all in as a matter of course. John had already been done for *Last Exit to Brooklyn.* Charles had crossed the boys in blue over reprinting *Fanny Hill* and been in the dock in Edinburgh. Tuppy's materials for the Diary were seized: her brief, the late Sir David Napley, got them back and got her off on the basis the boys from the Met were allowed to keep her magazines for their personal and private gratification. Jim had offended the authorities on a regular basis and been arraigned before the courts over the trifling matter of a naked blonde in a wheelchair at the 1963 Drama Conference at the Edinburgh Festival. And Anthony Wedgwood Benn had sworn a warrant for my own arrest under the 1967 Marine Broadcasting Offences Act.

Of course, if we had wanted to do something really subversive there was the brainpower and intellect and, in those days, the financial resources to pull off a major coup arrayed around that table.

What always fascinated me about John at Frankfurt was how he seemed to know everybody and he was always generous about sharing his contacts. Naturally, he knew every truly literary publisher in the world and could always come up with the name of, say, a Peruvian publisher who might be interested in rights in a very British novel. Sometimes his intrinsically generous and helpful nature got him into difficulties.

He told me the story of how, one year, Maurice Girodias arrived at the Fair completely penniless (or markless, I suppose). After a few nights, John got fed up with Girodias sleeping on the floor of his hotel room and devised a plan to move him on. On the third day of the Fair, John started a Frankfurt rumor: a Frankfurt rumor typically spreads like wildfire and within hours assumes the status of A Fact. The rumour was that Maurice was writing his own sensational autobiography. By the end of the day, more to Maurice's surprise than John's, world rights were sold and Maurice was – temporarily – rich. And off the floor of John's hotel room.

Although we were all resourceful and – in varying degrees – able, there can be little room for disputation. John was the intellectual heavyweight: almost universally looked up to in the publishing business as both inspired and inspiring. In the end of the day, the vast majority of us will be but minor footnotes in literary history. John will indubitably make it into a chapter heading.

Odile Hellier

When I first opened the fall 1998 issue of *Frank Magazine*, the first thing that caught my eye was a photograph of John Calder with the Editor, David Applefield. In the photo John is facing the camera, smiling at you, a mischievous smile more challenging than inviting. Under his arm, a battered typewriter – a tool and a symbol. The perfect portrait of one of a vanishing breed of publishers.

John Calder is a publisher unique in a trade which has turned into a vulgar commercial endeavor where profitability is the ruling word, and the author a mere commodity.

I do not have a clear recognition of the very first time I met this celebrated publisher of Beckett, but I remember well and with affection when Maurice Girodias (who had also published Beckett in the 1950s) and Calder would meet in my bookshop, The Village Voice. It was the mid-eighties and these two publishers of vision, who had both known better times, jokingly ironized about their promising past and the disappointing pitfalls of the present.

John's visits to the bookshop became regular – a ritual – and I felt very privileged that a publisher of his stature would come himself to check which of his titles had vanished from my shelves. Until the day I understood that John was visiting bookshops the world over making sure his authors were represented on the best shelves. Instead of feeling disappointed, my admiration for him jumped by a great leap. In times when the image of a publisher is one of a businessman sitting at his desk checking profits and measuring authors by the amount of money they bring in, John Calder was travelling the world over to share with booksellers his convictions and to get the books out to the public. And no huge suitcases needed either. No sooner had he entered the bookshop then he goes to the strategic shelves and pulls out his tiny, tiny pocket notebook, covering its pages with hieroglyphics only he can decipher. John travels light, all in his head and in his pocket. His blue striped suit (the only one I ever saw him wearing, is bulging with all kinds of notebooks, bits of paper, credit cards, which like so many narratives of his life, spill out of numerous pockets. More often than not I am more in the mood of listening to the harassing and cautions of my bank balance than to his seductive and convincing descriptions of the titles he wants to sell. But he never shows disappointment or frustration and, right there before leaving the shop, buys two or three books, thus increasing his own personal library. His place calls to mind for me a literary gem: *Too Loud a Solitude* – a novel by Bohumil Hrabal in which the protagonist has a job reducing books to pulp; from the belt which carries the books to their destruction, our hero sneakily snatches away one world masterpiece after another. At home he piles these masterpieces on sagging shelves which ultimately collapse on our hero, who lies buried beneath the world's greatest works of intelligence and imagination. John reads more than anyone I know, some 900 pages a week, the equivalent of three to five books. He also writes constantly – memoirs, reviews and obituaries. John's famous obituaries! How often have I smiled, as he would tell me of yet another famous personality not yet dead, whose obituary he had already written and submitted to the commissioning newspaper.

John the publisher and John the gypsy-scholar – all the time on the move. When he is not travelling to sell his books, he flies overnight to some distant city to experience the thrill and ecstasy of a new production of some opera he must already have seen twenty times.

A man of passions but also of convictions who, during the heated debate over the Net Book Agreement, fought both tooth and nail not only to defend the interests of the independent publishers, but also those of the independent bookseller. John's fighting spirit, much needed to survive in a trade of complex rights and shark attacks, more often than not gets him mired in lawsuits. That reminds me of William Gaddis' fabulous satire of today's world of *plaideurs* – *A Frolic of His Own*. Those lawsuits are like punctuation marks in the turbulent story of his life as a publisher.

John is definitely unique: a Man of Letters and an aesthete with a great appetite for life, but who, like Samuel Beckett, his author and friend, knows the futility of it all. Life is a joke and a great sense of humour, albeit Beckettian, is the best secret to ride it out. And, no doubt, John has got plenty of it: a B+ one – Beckettian plus British.

Alors, right on John and joyeux anniversaire! In place of the boring traditional couplet – *un grand éclat de rire!*

IMEC ARCHIVES

Ledlanet, The Calder Estate

"He inhabits a bridge between the two worlds, over which he scampers naughtily in both directions...**"**

– Victor Herbert

Victor Herbert

Something naughty. That's what John Calder always seems to be up to, at least when I've been around him. He has a sly smile for all occasions (probably in proper appreciation of the follies of mankind) but that smile has the camouflage quality of naughty clever English students at Eton. In this case John is the naughty Scottish *enfant terrible*. Even when just having lunch, especially when just having lunch, he always grabs the bill with the sweeping motion of the perfect host, but his smile silently screams: "Let me put this on my company so that the rate payers of Britain (most of whom don't buy books) can pay 40% of our lunch, including that delicious brandy."

I first met John somewhere in the 60s. He had just made national headlines because a nude woman participated in the Drama Conference for the 1963 Edinburgh International Festival. Maybe you'll get a better report elsewhere in this Festschrift. Anyway, this was before being clothed became optional in the UK and John has immediate guest privileges in the counterculture.

John was, and still is, more at home with 19th century Mozart and Wagner and the literary revolt of post World War II than with rock and roll, but I think he takes pleasure in being accepted by both the old and the new. He inhabits a bridge between the two worlds, over which he scampered naughtily in both directions while becoming one of the key publishers of his time.

I was a marginal partner when he took over Better Books on Charing Cross Road. Before the 60s changed all he rules, this was the only London west-end bookshop that held readings and literary activities. It was full of 19th century tiny interlocking rooms, cozy for browsing, but in the end, they were the cause of his own demise. Years later I met the original owner who explained the reason he sold the bookstore to John was that everyone in town who was both edu-

62 SHEIL ROAD
LIVERPOOL 8
Saty

To

JOHN CALDER, TWERP, BOGUS "INTELLECTUAL"

Has the Edinburgh Festival sunk so low under your Control that you have to descend to showing bare-arsed prostitutes?

Filthy Scum, I hope you and the wretched harlot that you exploited are properly dealt with

You ought to be thrown into the Sea No respect for anything – You are a Striking Symbol of a modern trend – immoral degraded beatniks – dirty minded toads, Your type ridicule all that is Sound, good, elevating etc and wallow in your self made Pig-Styes and think yourselves "intellectuals" – "avant-gardes" etc. You're just unbelieving, nasty immoral Scum. Yours disgustedly Kimberley

Get Your mind washed WITH CARBOLIC

128

cated and broke and who needed a few quid knew how easy it was to steal a few books from those tiny rooms. Everyone in London knew this...except John.

I do not know the Scottish John Calder *in situ.* I only know him south of the border, where he played the traditional role of a Scotsman having a better time in London than the locals. He was always surrounded by the most interesting people du jour and we all thought the party would go on forever. I suspect he published some of his writers just because they were literarily (if not literally) naughty and he wanted his imprint to certify his share of naughtiness. Of course, John always hid behind the unguardable quality of his authors.

I now know John west of the border. I see him when he whirlwinds through California, selling obscure books to local booksellers who cannot resist his charm. Now that he pays USA taxes (???) I protect my country from his tax depredations by forcing him to eat chez moi. Sometimes I think that on the way back to his hotel he orders some food that he has no room for...just so he can get one more tax-deductible receipt and stick it to the taxpayers one more time.

OHNER KRALLER - WESPENNEST

Harold Hobson

Harold Hobson

> **" "** I have known Mr. Calder for several years; there are few among my professional acquaintances about whose character I have formed such definite opinions. Mr. Calder is a man of absolute integrity. His catholic and adventurous taste in literature has led him to publish some of the most decisive books of our time. His courage is unshakable: nothing will move him from what he thinks to be right. I would put a child in his care and my bank account into his keeping. **" "**

– From a letter to The Times Literary Supplement, December 26, 1963, from Harold Hobson, London Sunday Times theatre critic.

LEPHONE REGENT 1985

TELEGRAPHIC ADDRESSES
INLAND: BOOKDOM, LONDON W.1
CABLES: BOOKDOM, LONDON W.1

JOHN CALDER (Publishers) LTD.

DIRECTORS: JOHN CALDER   MARION BOYARS
LESLEY MACDONALD   ROY JONES F.A.C.C.A.

17 SACKVILLE STREET, PICCADILLY, LONDON, W.I

JMC/AH

J. Haynes, Esq.,
The Traverse Theatre,
Lawnmarket,   30th October, 1964.
EDINBURGH 1.

Dear Jim,

      Please try and get a decision out of Harewood
as quickly as possible regarding the four-author play
for the Traverse.   Every day is precious if it is to
be ready by July.   Arden has already agreed provided he
does not have to be the first one.   My idea at present
is as follows:-

1.   Peter Weiss.
2.   Ionesco.
3.   Arden.
4.   Tennessee Williams or some such.

alternatively:-

3.   Dewey.
4.   Arden.

Yours,

John.

CHARLES MAROWITZ

Charles Marowitz

*A*nthropomorphic gnome. Hiberian troll. Extra-galactic android from the planet Kultur beyond Ursa Major. Lord of the Manner. Master of the Revels. Reverend of the Irreverent. Calderon de la Barker. Man of La Munchers. Great Scot!

These are some of the terms that reel into the brain when contemplating John Calder. In all of them, I sense the impulse to reconcile irreconcilables and make an equation between something small and something grandiose. Like the tiny seed from which the oak springs, or the pea-sized key which when deflected on the keyboard brings the galaxies of the World Wide Web swimming into one's ken.

Memories of John, like the attempt at nomenclature, are diffuse and unassemblable.

I recall being in the Soho office and casually mentioning that Peter Brook was contemplating a production of the *Marat/Sade* at the RSC and then seeing the idea slither into John's brain like a slug into a pregnant slot machine; the telephones activated; commands issued; the manuscript contracted.

John in his kilt playing Sol Hurok in the highlands; displaying the kind of rarefied culture that make typical Scots barf up their Drambuie. John at the Edinburgh Drama Conference contemplating the chaos of England's first real live happening: a nude on a trolley, Carol Baker climbing over rows of seats, Kenneth Tynan's stutter being guyed on tape. John's Cheshire-cat smile mooning across the Usher Hall, wondering how, when it was all over and done with, the church elders would be sharpening their snickersnees to have a go at his testicles. The smile smiling on unperturbed.

In Edinburgh and in London, we shared a lot of things – even girlfriends – without rancor – without spite. Gillian One in Million had enough grace to temper wily New York Jews and sawed off Scots litterateurs. The nourishment was mutual and happily, sequential rather than simultaneous. One wondered what deep dark secrets were exchanged over midnight cups of scented tea; what affinities were proven.

That he revered great writing is a truism; that he mustered the super-human tolerance required to put up with great writer's quiddities (Trocchi's truculence, Burroughs' erraticism, Ionesco's eccentricity) is perhaps less appreciated. When he found Beckett, he found a great purpose to his life. He was as much an acolyte as he was a guardian and a champion. His understanding of Beckett opened hidden waterways in his own nature which made it possible to launch other vessels similarly touched by the Irishman's genius. Assimilating Beckett gave John the eye to ferret out uncategorizable, off-beat British writers and helped stoke the mini-revolution he instigated on Wardour Street.

Being raised a Scot and yet assimilating in London, he understood cant and watched hypocrisy blossom into the tainted verdure which was England in the 60s and 70s. As both a publisher and an enlightened 20th century spirit, he recognized that censorship was merely a buttoned-up, stiff upper lip form of primeval diabolism and that it must be constantly assailed if Salem were not to come again. In fighting those battles, he sensed that he was dismantling windmills which were as much a part of his own upbringing as they were offshoots of a naturally repressive culture. There were meetings and conferences, acts of public defiance and the manning of many barricades. Throughout, he believed it was the Word which had to keep the Word free and that books were simply rivets strengthening the armour of the just warriors.

You could converse with John in a theatre lobby, in a pub, or over a tastefully ordered dinner in an up-market Soho restaurant and walk away with the impression that he was congenitally inane. But in a searing public phrase or courageous public act, you then had to reconcile the actions and the manner and in so doing, were forced to conclude the obtuseness was all on your side. That grit and daring, perceptiveness and insight could co-habit with that which appeared to be curiously gormless.

The answer to all the Establishment flak, the riposte to the heavies who would have him change his ways and refrain from giving offense was the Calderian giggle. A tippling little chortle of compressed air between his squinty eyes and quivering nostrils which reduced the

MR. CALDER TAKES A CIVIL LIBERTY

LONDONER'S Diary

Mr. John Calder's attempts to publicise next Monday's Gala Evening Concerning Depravity and Corruption may have enmeshed him in complications with the Metropolitan Police.

The poster, advertising the star encrusted entertainment organised by the National Council for Civil Liberties and the Defence of Literature and the Arts Society, of which Mr. Calder is secretary, has been adjudged too sexy—or perhaps too recondite — for London Transport travellers.

His most effective means of display prohibited, Mr. Calder decided to take a slight civil liberty himself. He made his way round the West End in the early hours of today, pasting up the posters.

SPOTTED

Mr. Calder was found by the police at 3.45 a.m. in Panton Street, near the Comedy Theatre, having put up about a dozen of the posters.

He told me today: "I was spotted by this chap who seemed to be just passing, and who seemed to take an objection to civil liberties or something. He called the police from a box in Cambridge Circus. About three or four minutes later, a big van, with about five or six officers in uniform — I fancy one was an inspector — appeared, and cautioned me.

"They told me I would be summoned." So far, however, there has been no word from the police about what proceedings, if any, are being brought.

The poster, designed by Alan Aldridge, shows a long coiled snake, with a naked girl and man forming the end of the tail.

man to a naughty little child; a child who cocked his snook at the philistine self-righteousness which was always out to get him.

John's place in the pantheon is secure. He's up there alongside Sylvia Beach, Maurice Girodias and Barney Rossett. One only prays that as the carnivorous and insatiable appetite of cyberspace threatens to swallow the written word whole, there will be future successors to the stubborn, individualistic and idiosyncratic publisher that he epitomizes.

Claudia Menza

Claudia Menza

John had conceived this notion, you see. No surprise there. He was forever coming up with some plan or other. The office was alive with agendas and schedules, lists and tallies, notes which might remind him to return a phone call or stand for Parliament, limn the first few lines of a poems or outline a complete strategy to save the arts from the hands of the Philistines. With every step you ran the risk of grinding into the carpet, John's latest method of dealing with ambush, each scribbled note a foray into battle, a small shield against what he – quite rightly – perceived to be a war between artists and money-lenders, each sheet a hedge against the encroaching enemy, making up in number what they lacked in durability.

"I'm working out a play," John announced as I opened the door one morning.

John rarely engages in small talk. He often wastes no time with such niceties as "Good morning," but seems always to be continuing a conversation, as if you had just returned from the loo.

"It's to be called 'The Claudia and Charles Show.' I'm taking some of your work – poems, monologues – and some of Charles' work – his philosophical writings, parts of his novels – and putting them together in a piece which will tell something of your individual preoccupations while talking about your life together as writers and as an interracial couple living in the United States."

I stood in the doorway, the key still in my hand. It was November 1992. My husband, Charles Frye, had been diagnosed with cancer a month earlier. John had said little about this, save a few abrupt queries as to Charles' state of mind, our plans for his cure, how we were getting on. I was frankly grateful for his brusque manner, as I was already weary of the earnest questions, the gush of hands, well-meaning overtures that merely fanned the flames beginning to lick at my

JOHN&JOHN

John Calder & Photographer John Minihan

heart. I could not bear another anxious face, difficult as it was to compose my own, the one inside, grieving despite the positive prognosis we had received. Charles was undergoing natural treatments to build up his immune system, an effort to outrun the cancer which wanted him for its own.

"A play?" I said. "Oh John, that's so sweet of you."

"Nothing to do with it," John snorted. "Good exposure for your work. Build up a following. Besides, I need a new piece to go to the Cheltenham Festival with and this would be ideal." He stopped. "Well, are you coming in or are you going to stand in the doorway all morning? It's already 9:30. Some of us have been here since 7:00 a.m. working out various bits. All I need from you is the odd piece which I haven't been able to find."

There was no doubt he had tried, though. I saw my desk as through a mist: files opened, drawers pulled out, a copy of my book The Lunatics Ball and Charles' From Egypt to Don Juan: The Anatomy of Black Philosophy held open by pink rocks Charles and I had gathered at Cape Cod one summer. John's own desk resembled an archaeological site. He was working in a hole at the centre, surrounded by half-pieces of paper scattered like shards from the dig. A copy of my earlier book of poems was under his left foot and Charles' latest manuscript lay spread out on the floor. John was wielding a pair of scissors in one hand and a stapler in the other, while choosing at random, it seemed, a quarter-page here and a jotted note there and stapling them together with a resounding crunch.

I walked in and hung up my coat. "Who's going to perform it? I asked, the reality of a play, a fait accompli. "Your actors from the Theatre of Literature?"

John had been transposing a group of brilliant and rather cheerless novels into play formats, the result of which I had dubbed, "The John Calder Grim Theatre Series."

"You are," said John. "You and Charles. I've seen *you* perform. Quite good. A little direction needed. Not much. Touch here and there. We'll be in London two days," he continued, "Then straight on to Cheltenham and travelling for about two weeks after that. Four to six performances, I should think." He paused. "By the way does Charles have any acting experience?"

I smiled. Charles was a tall, imposing figure, an academic whose soft, insistent voice and dignified magical demeanor either drove students to drop his classes immediately or sent them scurrying to the front of the room to sit at his feet. "He's like fucking Bodhisattva!" one of our friends had once exclaimed.

"I really don't know," I told John.

"Well, can he take direction?" John persisted.

I giggled. Can you direct the Bodhisattva?

In October, one year later, Charles and I and John were on a Virgin Atlantic flight bound for London. Charles had gotten the okay from his doctor, a new doctor, one who had placed fine hope in his chemotherapy treatments. Our London date had been put back and now our first performance in front of an audience would be in Cheltenham. John had counted on ironing out the kinks before the Festival, a gathering which would include many literary lights, most of whom he knew. Now he was having us rehearse mid-flight. Charles voice could barely be heard above the engines and John was becoming visibly nervous, gulping Cabernet Sauvingnon between each direction, pulling his glasses on and off, fumbling in his bulging jacket pockets to drag out a bit of tissue or to check the time of our performance once again in his beloved diary. An hour and a half into a very smooth flight, John's script had wine stains on it.

We rehearsed again in John's London office for two days. The London office, aside from the difference in personnel, looked exactly like the New York office: open file cabinets, cartons of books, and stacks of inventory printouts, all of which seemed to indicate a recent move or imminent flight. In between coffee and sandwiches, John was ever the patient director, the very essence of understanding and sympathy, often saying the lines himself to point out inflection or emphasis. Charles listened intently then made such infinitesimal adjustments you would have needed sonar to detect them. John was clearly distraught but hell bent on not showing it. "Yes, well, right," he'd say to Charles each time Charles re-read a line. And while they were bent over lines, I kept up my diary tracking Charles illness: the rare smile, which I celebrated, his small complaints which I knew masked groundswells of pain and sorrow.

The morning of our third day, we climbed – and I use the term advisedly – into John's car, which resembled a lawn mower in size and sound. Charles sat in the front seat with his head down or looking out the side window because John was driving with one hand and with the other running his finger along a map which he had spread over the steering wheel. I was crammed in the back seat between valises, a bag of shoes, and an overnight case. There was no room in the boot: it was filled with boxes of catalogues, order forms, and copies of Beckett and Artaud and Duras and Celine titles, just in case we happened to bump into a bookshop on our way to well – anywhere.

We arrived at Cheltenham at 1:00. It was a beautiful autumn day, still warm with a slight edge to the air. John had put us up at a handsome hotel at which the House of Windsor stayed when, I suppose, they fancied a bit of poetry. There were posters of Charles and me displayed prominently on the Festival grounds, a recent photograph showing a hopeful Charles and a Claudia whose face was threaded with grief. Below that was the snappy copy John had written, although not quite as snappy as John's catalogue description of one of his books which read, "Horny Irish medical student on the rampage." We were to meet John for yet another rehearsal at 2:30. Our performance was that evening.

John was pacing when we arrived, that is, walking back and forth in short, contemplative bursts that made him look as if he were being continuously shot out of a cannon.

"Right," he said when we walked in. "I will introduce you and you will walk in on 'I give you Claudia and Charles.' Smile when you look at the audience, and try to be relaxed."

I smiled then and there. I've never met a chance to perform that I didn't like. Charles cleared his throat, his indication that he had heard what you said but didn't necessarily give it any credence.

At 5:00 we returned to our room. I took a shower then my requisite pre-performance whisky. Charles napped. I watched his face relax in dreams, the grooves of fear erased by sleep's loving hand. I thought about the play, this woven thing, this record of our life, our daily chit-chat which John had loomed from years of listening to us, and to which we had added here and there a phrase, a favoured word, fillips to lines which then sounded, if not exactly like us, so close that we had begun to quote from the scripts as if from ourselves.

At 7:30, we walked across a common to the hall. The dusk still held a spark of light. Charles was wearing a dark suit and his customary matching tie and pocket handkerchief. I was wearing the ivory suit I had been married in. John was waiting in the front row, pen and script at the ready. We had a formal handshake. The room became quiet. John stepped to the stage and we followed on cue.

I did not recognize the actor with whom I played that night. He

141

joked, he produced asides, his hands found gestures in thin air. In fact, he ad libbed so much, I turned to him at one point and said, "Is there any hope of getting back to the script?" He turned benevolently toward the audience and said, "Of course, Sweetie! No matter how far afield we go, we always come back to us."

And then it was over and we were bowing. A couple of people actually gave us a standing ovation, but the first one up was John, who had dropped the script and was rushing toward the stage and toward Charles, whom he hugged headlong in a wash of gladness and relief.

"You were magnificent!" he told Charles, ignoring me completely. "Absolutely magnificent! What happened? How did you do it and where did you find that voice?"

"It was in the script," said Charles, returning to his somber self. "Besides," he added with a little trickster smile, "I always save the best for last."

And so he had. And so had John.

Charles died the following October. Sometimes I look at our marked up scripts, our life annotated. I follow the lines to live them again, to hear the song once more. I see John's own hand in inserts and transpositions, an arranger who took melody and made music.

Karl Orend

John Calder was and remains for me the most influential and important independent literary publisher active in Britain since the war. The fortunes of his house have been in a sense a mirror of the values of society and literary thought over the recent decades. No matter what vicissitudes of fortune beset him he is for thousands like myself a pivotal influence on both our intellectual and personal lives.

I first read Calder books as a teenager in a remote Fenland town in the east of England. The books John published were uniformly important and opened my eyes to both literature and the world. Many of the discoveries he gave me have remained tremendously influential and are works I return to again and again. From Beckett to Wyndham Lewis, from Goethe and Morike to Borges, Burroughs, Claude Simon and Henry Miller there has been a constant factor in all my reading life – the presence of John Calder's books. I have never been tempted to resell one and have never doubted the value of anything that bore his imprint. I cannot say as much for anyone else. My father would drive me forty miles to Cambridge once a month to see what new fruit the tree had borne – Calder books were sometimes hard to find but I would search without regret, somehow knowing that the man who made these books would help to shape me and allow me the freedom of an international education that could never come from school.

When, many years later, I met John, I realized for the first time the enormity of what he had achieved and also his tremendous integrity, loyalty and fighting spirit. He not only defended countless books in court, virtually bankrupting himself in the process – but he fought for all – the famous and the unknown in equal measure. He fought so that you and I could read the books we choose, and the authors would know that if their book had merit, no matter how absurd the laws of obscenity, they would never lack a champion. Two years ago one of my books was banned in England – a book by Aragon, Peret and Man Ray deemed obscene – only John, instinctively and without thought for himself, offered to stand up and fight in my corner. How little so many young people realize when they read Miller, Selby, Burroughs, even Duras' *The Lover* and so much of modern writing, there would never have been the opportunity to do so without this man? How many realize that many of France and Germany's great post-war writers owe their presence in the Anglophone world largely to his efforts; Heinrich Boll, Martin Walser, Wolfgang Bochert, Jean-Paul Sartre, Robbe-Grillet, Eluard, Queneau, Helene Cioux, Nathalie Sarraute and Raymond Radiguet to name but a few. No one seems to agree how many Nobel winners John has published – anywhere between 15 and 20 – but the numbers are not important – he published them all, from Ivo Andric and Beckett to Canetti before their fame, before they entered the canon, at a time when no one else in the English speaking world would touch them.

Time is not necessarily kind to men of genius and with the passing of many of his great authors the literary estates have chosen money over loyalty, and lured to giant conglomerates the now successful authors which John Calder fostered in obscurity. The bookshop culture has undergone a revolution where W.H. Smiths, Waterstones and Dillions control the vast majority of outlets. Their terms for small publishers are crippling and though their staff may be burdened with at least a bachelors degree a piece they show an often amazing (though not suprising) lack of education. I remember ten years ago in Nottingham when I arranged to meet John for lunch he turned up two hours early – turned away from each shop in turn without an order; in his struggle to go on, John was forced to rep his own books and invest his all in an attempt to keep them alive. Is there not something sad in this world when a man who brought so much greatness into our lives, who invested his life in the dissemination of great literature, can be turned away by a twenty-two year old who has never heard of Alexander Trocchi let alone Yevtushenko and Robert Pinget. I know the feeling well – I was once turned down at Waterstone's, Charing Cross Road, for one copy of Henry Miller's *Mezzotints* collected for the first time together since Henry and June peddled them door to door in 1920's New York. That is one reason why John Calder stood up to defend the Net Book Agreement – to protect the small independent publishers and booksellers who were there for the love of books and communication, the defense of literature above all else.

The tide may be against us – my own publishing efforts will amount to nothing beside John's – I have neither the courage nor the heart in such a world as this – but one thing I know – that all those who value the great literatures of the world owe a great debt to this man, to his courage and gentle kindness – to all those who share his love of culture in all its artistic, musical and literary forms I ask that for all our sakes you buy his books, rediscover the treasures he has given us and celebrate the example and the values he has shared. There is no better guide.

Karl Orend is Director of Alyscamps Press Paris and co-director of Carrefour Press founded in 1929, in Paris by Michael Fraenkel and Walter Lownefels.

LEDLANET   MILNATHORT   KINROSS-SHIRE

Ledlanet Nights **Spring** *Summer*

FESTIVAL SEASON

- OPERA
- CONCERTS
- FOLK SONGS
- CEILIDH
- MEMBERS' NIGHTS
- BALLS

10th YEAR

RESTAURANT   BAR   BUFFET

Ledlanet First Night

Fond memories of Beethoven's bi-centenary

> Exploding dustbins in the grounds
> (Such proto-Bonapartic sounds
> Were, like the lighting, less than more on cue)
> Made Beethoven rip up his page
> Of dedication, quit the stage,
> Rush up the stairs and in a rage
> Upbraid the switchboard guy (I wonder who?)
>
> That kilted laird, somewhat aghast,
> Fair reeled as the unscripted blast
> Drowned out the E-flat B-flat E-flat theme
> Of the Eroica. And all
> Who'd gathered in Ledlanet's hall
> Were stunned as from behind the wall
> "It's all a fucking shambles!" came the scream.

John Rushby-Smith

The sound guy

John Calder devised and wrote the script for homage to Beethoven which was performed at Ledlanet in 1970. At the time I was working for BBC Radio, and at John's request I used some spare studio time to put together a tape of musical and dramatic excerpts which were played in at various salient moments during the production. John had engaged the wonderful actor Patrick Wymark to play Beethoven, but Patrick got the script rather too late to learn it, so had to read it from a lectern. Little "inky" spotlights were provided for him to read by, but J.C. insisted on operating the lighting switchboard (a primitive affair) himself, and the cues got so far out of sync that Patrick spent much of his time in total darkness. Unpredictable, electrically-fired maroons, suspended in dustbins outside the house, were used to rep-

the diary

The very first entry in John's collection of opera diaries where he records every performance he's ever seen.

resent advancing Napoleonic armies and added to the confusion.

Things came together better on subsequent evenings, and there was a wonderful night at Ledlanet following a performance when Patrick, who by now had become convinced he *was* Beethoven, insisted that I should accompany violinist Leonard Friedman in some of 'his' Violin Sonatas (Leonard led a string quartet that was also part of the production.) We went on to play through a movement for violin and piano which I had written some 10 years before, and Leonard promised that if I wrote two more movements to make up a sonata he would play it with me at a Ledlanet Nights concert. This came to fruition a year later and was both the most uplifting and the most terrifying moment of my musical life. Uplifting because the opportunity to have an artist of Leonard's calibre perform my music was a revelatory privilege, and terrifying because I had never presumed to present myself as a concert pianist. Never have I sweated so much!

Alas neither Patrick nor Leonard is with us any more, but I still have a tape of that performance and whenever I play it I am fondly reminded of the debt I owe them, and especially John Calder, for the inspiration that so broadened my musical career. John, I salute and thank you.

John Rushby-Smith
Composer & Record Producer

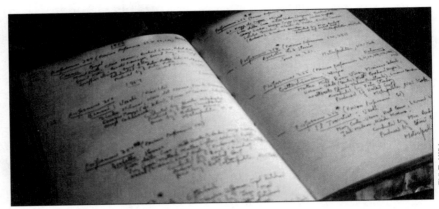

AMY LAND

❝ John Calder went to the opera 80 times in 1996. John Calder has attended 2,877 opera performances in his life (up to the 3rd of January, 1997, 783 different operas). ❞

– E.D.

Irving Wardle

Whatever the failings of millionaire art patrons, they tend as a breed to have staying power. Also, by starting from the position of wordly fulfillment they are not susceptible, as hunger artists are, to the eroding effects of success. The English cultural scene would be drastically impoverished if you subtracted the contribution of men like Barry Jackson, Terence Gray, Philip Sassoon, and Lord Berners – or coming up to date, Eddie Kulukundis, and Ernest Hall. It may no longer be strictly accurate to include John Calder in their company – one of the glories of his career being his readiness to send a Canadian logging fortune up in smoke to launch Ionesco, Beckett and Artaud in this country. But money or not money, his career over the past 40 years has shown the staying power of a Medici.

I first met him in the early 1960s through an Oxford pal, Arthur Boyars (a hunger artist if there ever was one) who also advised me to watch my step on the way up to the office, as the stairs were booby-trapped with reels of Calder-financed opera films. I knew nothing of Calder's other life as an impresario, or even whether those films were ever shown; but the books were pouring out, and he let me into that world. The money was peanuts; but he gave me access to print along with people like Lindsay Anderson, John Arden and Conor O'Brien. Later on, it became a custom to moan about the miserly rates he paid to authors and translators. As a contributor and one-time editor on the Calder payroll, I have no complaints. The point then was to get the new authors and print while they were still hot; and to catch the mood of the time on the wing in publications like the *International Theater Annual* and *Gambit*.

When I was editing *Gambit* a few years later we published Heathcote Williams's amazing piece *AC/DC*. Heathcote wanted a different type-face for each character; and it was discovered that this

151

could be done with a fancy IBM machine, but the cost would wipe out the author's and the editor's fees combined. Heathcote and I immediately agreed to this. Not through indifference to money, but because the work was important and this was the only way of getting it out. Nobody ever complained about writing for nothing for *Encore*. It would have been different if Calder himself had been on the make; but manifestly, he was driven by a greed that no balance sheet could ever satisfy. He was greedy for art and greedy for freedom. When I first met him, and heard that guardedly inexpressive voice, he gave the impression of a recently escaped prisoner, obsessively on the look-out for shackles and prison yards of ordinary life. His manner embodied the slogan that the price of liberty is eternal vigilance; and maybe the books would have been fewer, the publishing house shorter-lived if he had dropped his guard against the perceived threat of Britain's philistines and moral police (a view corroborated by one ex-girlfriend who fondly remembered him as "Twinkletoes.")

That was in the 1960s, when there was no lack of freedom campaigners; nor, indeed, of unmercenary aesthetes and Beckett and Artaud enthusiasts. This was before publishing in this country became a branch of accountancy and the artists of the 1960s proceeded on their separate routes into affluent compromise and defeated silence. Not to labour the point, the scene is altered; except in Paris, where I last met Calder in 1996. Since he left England all I'd heard of him was what he wrote in his Obituaries for *The Independent*. Obituaries in the 1980s were one of the growth areas of British journalism; and Calder's were among the best written, best researched and most judicious of the lot – especially when he was writing about members of the Franco-American literary demi-monde who had never before received serious treatment in the British Press. From reading these pieces I suppose I was expecting to meet some elder statesman figure, sagely looking back on the troubled world from which he had now withdrawn. When I did see him, the twenty year gap closed up as if it had never been. He looked a bit heavier, but otherwise he was exactly the same urgent, seldom-smiling, hospitable presence, with a stack of new projects to impart and a suitcase of books (I think he had around 500 on his list at that time) to deliver. Time stood still. The Parisian background faded away and it was as if he was still hatching plans with his back to the wall in the Brewer Street office. At that time he was teaching philosophy classes and completing a book on Beckett besides pounding the bookshop beat as a publisher with wares to

sell. I have never been a close friend of Calder's; but I came away from that meeting very pleased to have known him at all; the uncorrupted survivor of a good time. For 35 years he has been a feature of the cultural landscape – simultaneously taking a sledge-hammer to the clubmanship of the British arts scene, while himself resisting every pressure towards change and compromise. He looked to me like a man who had never given himself a day of peace and was fated to go to his grave unsatisfied. How lucky for the rest of us that a few such people exist.

Tim Waterstone

John Calder has cornered the market for obituaries of literary folk. He does them very well. Signed or unsigned they are equally as obviously from his pen. No one in our time has been a more perceptive observer of a certain part of the scene. Himself a maverick, he likes his mavericks, though he has no feel at all for popular and commercial publishing of whatever kind. But his own Calder world of badly typed catalogues, devotion beyond devotion to his authors (particularly Samuel Beckett certainly, who returned the loyalty, but what a list it has been over the years!…Claude Simon, Ionesco, Pirandello, Sarraute…) preparing to die, or at very least to be imprisoned, heroically and hopelessly, for the right to publish *Last Exit to Brooklyn,* publishers' travellers, dusty provincial independent booksellers with piles of books all over the floor – this world he knows better than anyone alive.

Of course that Calder world no longer exists really, at least in the form that John would like it to. He misses it. Now it's the slick world of Waterstone's and Borders megastores, and the clinical, unforgiving information technology we depend on that tells all and tells nothing. And maybe it's not always so slick after all. Still today, seventy-two years old, John trudges the four corners of the globe calling on bookshops and watching over his list. He still writes me twice a year, uninvited of course, with an astonishingly perceptive overview of every single one of our Waterstone's branches often uncomfortable reading. Sometimes unfair.

But he has an immediate eye for which booksellers and managers know books and love books and those who don't – in Waterstone's eyes, as well as John's, by far the most important qualities of all. Other aspects of good bookselling – occupancy costs, stock turn, sales per square foot, payroll productivity, shrink – John is impervious to.

A GALA BENEFIT

in aid of the

Free Art Legal Fund

**AN EVENING
OF MUSIC AND READING**
from the work of
SAMUEL BECKETT
and
BERTOLD BRECHT

SUNDAY, APRIL 30th, 1967.
ROYAL COURT THEATRE, S.W.1

" *Thank God he never thought of running a chain of bookshops himself.* "

– Tim Waterstone

Oblivious to. Thank God he never thought of running a chain of bookshops himself.

John fought and he's still fighting of course, a marvelous cause. He never stops. Particularly if he's going to lose. The Net Book Agreement. Marches down Whitehall in protest about Arts funding. Wrestling his authors' books into resistant bookshops. Anything whatsoever in defence of a book trade whose traditional values he loves, and which has not always been as cognisant as it should have been as to what John has done for us all. He's a true hero of mine. May he live forever.

WESPENNEST

❝❝He went for what he believed in...
and that what he believed in was
not always going to be best-selling
material, for which I admired him.❞❞

— Lord Harewood

Barbara Wright

"*A* remarkable achievement, a remarkable event, a remarkable record, a remarkable man," says Jim Haynes, inviting contributions to John's half-century-in-publishing Festschrift. Remarkable indeed. But I imagine that everyone who picks up this book will already know *something* about this remarkability, and I am sure that other contributors will be writing about it's philosophical aspects far better than I could. So I hope to be forgiven for just microcosming it, and simply trying to describe the effect John's remarkable activities have had on me and my "professional career" as a translator. My excuse is that one is always being enjoined to write about what one *really* knows...

I didn't ever imagine I could be a translator. In fact, I was working (a bit) as a piano accompanist (which I now realize is exactly the same sort of activity), when fate intervened in the form of Stefan and Franciszka Themerson, who founded the other fabulous independent avant-garde press, Gaberbocchus. Gaberbocchus was a very little "little" publisher – rather I think its initial capital consisted of a loan of one hundred pounds – but every one of its books was a one-off, chosen and designed with loving care. One day the Themersons casually asked me: "Would you like to translate *Ubu Roi?*" And I, equally casually, answered something like; "And sure why wouldn't I?"

That's a very long story. But the next book Gaberbocchus asked me to translate was Raymond Queneau's *Exercises in Style*. And somehow or other John Calder happened to get hold of a copy of the *Exercises*, and he thought it was Good. And he wanted to meet me. And he did. And he told me that it was his bedside book. And when it became out of print with Gaberbocchus he wanted to take it over. And Gaberbocchus didn't like the idea of anyone else messing about with our baby. John persevered, though with infinite tact, and no doubt plenty of what Robert Pinget so beautifully calls "psycho-psychi," and at (fairly long) last they finally said: Oh *all right*...

But in the meantime, John had been nursing me, and he gave me other books to translate: Robbe-Grillet's *Snapshots and Towards a New Novel*, Tzara's *Seven Dada Manifestos*... And when I suggested to the publisher who had brought out my translation of Queneau's *Zazie dans le Metro* that it might be a good idea to produce more Queneau translations - what about his first novel, *Le Chiendent*, for instance? – They weren't interested. But when I timidly mentioned it to John, he was immediately enthusiastic, and he brought it out as *The Bark Tree*. And then he published Queneau's *The Sunday of life*, and then Queneau's *The Flight of Icarus*, and then Queneau's *We Always Treat Women Too Well*...

John's extreme peculiarity is that he has *never* (so far as I know) published any book because it would (or might) make money. But he always (if at all possible) published any book he believed in, and thought should be given a chance. Hence his intoduction to the English public of all those then-unknown pioneer writers, both English and foreign, who are now household names. John is the English publishing equivalent of the French gallery owner Pierre Loeb, and the French metteur-en-scene Jean-Marie Serreau.

In the 40s and 50s Serreau staged, among other playwrights he believed in but who were then practically unknown, Beckett, Adamov, Ionesco. This idealism naturally caused him some financial hardship. (All these writers figure on John's list.) Pierre Loeb started his Galerie Pierre in the 1920s, and gave exhibitions to similar artists then at the very beginning of their careers. Giacometti – who at the time was in his early twenties; Miro and Max Ernst, in their early thirties; the Surrealists as early as 1925. All three, men of courage and vision.

Two of the writers John gave me to translate were Robert Pinget and Nathalie Sarraute, both of whom became real friends with whom I have spent many, many happy and enlightening hours. Robert would always patiently answer any questions that no other French friends could answer, but he was just a little bit too ready to say that everything was *superbe*. Nathalie Sarraute is the translator's ideal author. She knows English perfectly, and is vitally interested in every word of her translations. I go and read her the translation when I feel I can go no further. She follows with French. If she has a query, she will stop me and we will discuss. Sometimes we will decide that that really is the best that can be done. Sometimes she will not like something but I will defend it and she will say (roughly): Okay, you're the boss.

Sometimes we will both be somewhat dissatisfied, and she will come up with the perfect solution – in English. (She has denied this, but it is nothing but the truth.)

One of Nathalie Sarraute's tenets, of course, is that we are all multi-multifaceted. Once you think about it it becomes obvious, and should certainly be thought about more. But when we are working together, just two of her facets emerge. During the reading, she is entirely concentrated on the text and its problems, nothing else exists. But when we take a break – she is just a lovely lady there with me – we gossip and chuckle, and out come the vodka or whisky…(Although her glass of whisky is nine tenths Perrier water with about a half a centimeter of whisky on top…)

All this I owe to John. Thank you, John!

Samuel Beckett by Sorel Etrog

Books published by John Calder

Annotated bibliography
Prepared by Howard Aster and Amy Land

- Literature
- Beckett
- Music
- Politics
- Gambit International Theatre Forum
- Acorn Press

Bibliographic Guide:

Sequence

Author/ Title/ Translator/ Imprint/ Year/ Reprinted/ ISBN/ HC/ PB/ Category/ Pagination

Imprints

John Calder = JC
Calder & Boyars = C & B
Jupiter Books = J
Calder Publications = CP
Riverrun = R
John Calder (Publishers) Ltd = JCP
Spearman & Calder = S & C
Bookville = B
Acorn Press = AP
Evergreen Books = EB

Note: Imprints are catalogued as designated on the Title Page, not the copyright page or the spine

Categories

P = poetry
D = drama
F = fiction
NF = non-fiction
E = essays
M = memoirs
LC = literary criticism
H = history
B = biography
O = opera
M = music
MB = music biography

Literature

Anonymous, Her, C&B, 1972, 0 7145 0895 0 HC, F, pp.301

Adamov, Arthur, Paolo Paoli:The Years of the Butterfly, A Play in Twelve Scenes, trans. Geoffrey Brereton, JC, 1959 -------- HC/PB, D, pp.123

Adamov, Arthur, Ping Pong: Two Plays - Professor Taranne, trans. Peter Mayer, Ping Pong, trans. Derek Prouse, JC,1962,------ HC/PB, D, pp.126

Agee, James, The Collected Poems, Robert Fitzgerald ed.,C&B, 1972, 0 7145 0819 5 HC, 0 7145 0887 X PB, P, pp.180

Alarcon, Pedro Antonio de, Three-Cornered Hat(The), trans. H.F.Turner, JC ,1959,------- HC/PB, F, pp.134

Andrews, Lyman, Kaleidoscope, C&B ,1973, 0 7145 1024 6 PB, -----HC, P, pp.80

Anderson, Quentin, American Henry James(The), JC, 1958, -----------HC, NF, pp.370

Andric, Ivo, Devil's Yard, trans. Kenneth Johnstone, JC, 1964, --------HC, F, pp.125

Andric, Ivo, The Women From Sarajevo, trans. Joseph Hitrec, C&B, 1966, 0 7145 0615 X PB, --------HC, F, pp. 345

Antrobus, John, 'why bournemouth?' & other plays, C&B 1970 0 7145 0642 7 PB ----------HC, D, pp. 130

Antrobus, John, 'hitler in liverpool' & other plays, JC, 1983, 0 7145 3898 1 PB , D, pp.140

Antrobus, John, 'trixie & baba', C&B, 1969, -------------PB/HC, D, pp.98

Aragon, Louis, The Libertine, trans. Jo Levy, JC, 1987 /CP 1993, 0 7145 4104 4 HC, 0 7145 4020 X PB, F, pp. 185

Arden, Jane, 'vagina rex and the gas oven', C&B, 1971,0 7145 0796 2 HC, 0 7145 0797 0 PB, D, pp. 64

Arp, Jean (Hans), Collected French Writings - Poems, Essays, Memoroes, trans Joachim Neugroschel, ed. Marcel Jean, C&B, 1974, 0 7145 0853 5 PB, -----------HC, P/E/M, pp. 574

Arrabal, Fernando, FOUR Plays- Orison, The Two Executioners, Fando and Lis, The Car Cemetery, trans. Barbara Wright, JC, 1958------------PB, -----------HC, D, pp.160

Arrabal, Fernando, The Burial of the Sardine, trans. Patrick Bowles, C&B,1966, 0 7145 0147 6 PB, ----------------HC, D, pp. 106

Arrabal, Fernando, Plays Volume 1, Orison, The Two Executioners, Fando and Lis, The Car Cemetery, trans. Barbara Wright, JC, 1962, /1976, 0 7145 0449 1 HC, 0 7145 0450 5 PB, pp. 156

Arrabal, Fernando, Plays Volume 2, Guernica, The Labyrinth, The Tricycle, Picnic on the Battlefield, The Condemned Man's Bicycle, trans. Barbara Wright, C&B, 1967, JC, 1976, 0 7145 0451 3 HC, 0 7145 0452 1 PB, D, pp. 150

Arrabal, Fernando, Plays Volume 3 , The Architect and the Emperor of Assyria, The Grand Ceremonial, The Solemn Communion, trans Jean Benedetti & John Calder, C&B, 1970, 0 7145 0453 X HC, 0 7154 0472 6 PB, D, pp.260

Artaud, Antonin, The Death of Satan and Other Mystical Writings, trans. Alaistair Hamilton and Victor Corti, C&B; 1974, 0 7145 0979 5, PB, ------------HC, L, pp.90

Artaud, Antonin, The Theatre and Its Double, trans. Victor Corti, C&B, 1970, JC 1974, JCP, 1977/1981/1985/1989, CP,1993 0 7145 0702 4 HC, 0 7145 0703 2 PB, E , pp. 102

Artaud, Antonin, 'the cenci', trans. Simon Watson-Taylor,C&B, 1969, ----------
PB, ----------------HC, D, pp. 95

Artaud, Antonin, Collected Works; Volume One, trans. Victor Corti, C&B, 1968, JCP 1978, 0 7145 0169 7 HC, 0 7145 0170 0 PB, E, pp; 256

Artaud, Antonin, Collected Works, Volume Two, trans. Victor Corti, C&B 1971, 0 7145 0171 9 HC, 0 7145 0172 PB, E, pp.240

Artaud, Antonin, Collected Works, Volume Three, C&B, 1972, 0 7145 0778 4 HC, 0 7145 0779 2 PB, E, pp.260

Artaud, Antonin, Collected Works, Volume Four, trans. Victor Corti, C&B, 1974, 0 7145 0622 2 HB, 0 7145 0623 0 PB, E, pp.221

Atkins, John, Graham Greene, JC, 1957, ------------PB, B, pp.240

Atkins, John, Graham Greene, C&B, Revised Edition 1966, ------------------HC, B, pp.240

Atkins, John, Six Novelists Look At Society: An Inquiry Into the Social Views of Elizabeth Bowen, L.P.Hartley, Rosamund Lehman, Christopher Isherwood, Nancy Mitford, C.P.Snow, JC, 1977, 0 7145 3535 4, HC, 0 7145 3863 9, PB, LC, pp.284

Atkins, John, Aldous Huxley: A Critical Study, JC 1956, C&B, 1957, new revised ane enlarged edition, 0 7145 0081 X, HC, LC, pp.218

Atkins, John, George Orwell, JCP, 1954, C&B, 1971, 0 7145 0715 6 HC, 0 7145 0716 4 PB, LC, pp. 394

Atkins, John, Sex in Literature: Volume 1 The Erotic Impulse in Literature, C&B, 1970, 07145-0522-6, HC, 07145-0523-4, PB, pp410

Atkins, John, Volume 2, The Classical Expression of the Sexual Impulse, C&B, 1973, 0-7145-0919-1, HC, 0-7145-1138-2, PB, E, pp 348

Atkins, John, Sex in Literature, Volume 3, The Medieval Experience, JC, 1978, 0-7145-368-7, HC, 0-7145-3801-2, PB, E, pp. 378

Atkins, John, Sex in Literature Volume 4, High Noon: The Seventeenth and Eighteenth Centuries, 1982, 0-7145-3756-X, HC, 0-7145-3977-5, PB, E, pp. 370

Atkins, John, J.B. Priestley: The Last of the Sages, JC, 1981, 0-7145-3804-3, HC, 0-7145-3950-3, PB, B, pp. 295

Atkins, John, The British Spy Novel: Styles in Treachery, JC, 1984, 0-7145-3997-X, HC? 0-7145-4056-0, PB, LC, pp. 280

B

Barbaud, Pierre, Haydn, Trans. Katherine Sorley Walker, JC, 1959, -------, PB, MB, 192pp

Barker, Howard, The Breath of the Crowd, JC, 1986, 0 7145 4099 4, PB, P, pp.48

Barker, Howard, Collected Plays, Volume One, Claw, No End To Blame, Victory, The Castle, Scenes From An Execution, JC, 1990, 0-7145-4161-3, PB, D, pp. 305

Barker, Howard, Collected Plays, Volume Two, The Love of a Good Man,

The Possibilites, Brutopia, Rome, Uncle Vanya, Ten Dilemmas, CP, 1993, 0-7145-4182-6, PB, D, pp. 400

Barker, Howard, Collected Plays, Volume Three, The Power of the Dog, The Europeans, Women Beware Women, Minna, Judith, Ego in Arcadia, CP, 1996, 0-7145-4279-2, PB, D, pp. 325

Barker, Howard, Collected Plays Volume Four, The Bite of the Night, Seven Lears, The Gaoler's Ache, He Stumbled, The House of Correction, CP, 1998, 0-7145-4279-2, PB, D, pp. 392

Barker, Howard, Arguments for a Theatre, JC, 1989, reprinted 1990, 0 7145 4152 4 PB, D, pp. 92

Barker, Howard, Don't Exaggerate (desire and abuse), JC 1985, 0 7145 4076 5 PB, D , pp. 70

Barker, Howard, The Ascent of Monte Grappa, JC 1991, 0 7145 4202 4 PB, D, pp. 80

Barker Howard, Gary the Thief/ Gary Upright, JC 1987, 0 7145 4137 0 PB, D, pp. 87

Barker, Howard, Lullabies for the Impatient, JC 1988, 0 7145 4153 2 PB, D, pp. 71

Barker Howard, The Bite of the Night, JC 1988, 0 7145 4124 9 PB, D, pp. 90

Barker Howard, The Castle : Scenes from an Execution, JC 1985, 0 7145 4074 9 PB, D, pp. 90

Barker Howard, The Tortmann Diaries, JC 1996, 0 7145 4821 4 PB, D, pp.78

Barker, Howard, 'crimes in hot counties' : ' fair slaughter', JC, 1978, reprinted 1984, 0 7145 4046 3 PB, D, pp; 106

Barker, Howard, 'no end of blame: scenes of overcoming' , JC, 1981, 0 7145 3912 0 PB, D, pp. 56

Barker, Howard, The Europeans/Judith , JC 1990, 0 7145 4144 3 PB, D, pp.67

Barker, Howard, Fair Slaughter, JC 1978, 0 7145 3654 7 PB, D, pp. 49

Barker, Howard, 'the hang of the gaol' & 'heaven', JC 1982, 0 7145 3769 1 PB, D, pp.114

Barker, Howard, A Hard Heart, CP, 1992, 0 7145 4232 6, PB, D pp. 45

Barker, Howard, A Hard Heart/The Early Hours of a Reviled Man, CP, 1992, 0 7145 4228 8, PB, D, pp. 80

Barker, Howard, Hated Nightfall/Wounds to the Face, CP 1994, 0 7145 4270 9, PB, D, pp.80

Barker, Howard, The Last Supper, JC, 1988, 0 7145 4149 4 PB, D, pp. 56

Barker, Howard, 'the love of a good man':' all bleeding', JC, 1980, 0 7145 3767 5, PB, 0 7145 3802 7, HC ,D pp. 106

Barker, Howard, No End of Blame, JC, 1981, 0 7145 39120, PB, D, pp.55

Barker, Howard, two plays for the right/ 'the loud boy's life & 'birth on a hard shoulder', JC, 1982, 0 7145 3896 5, PB, D, pp. 123

Barker, Howard, 'that good between us' :/ ' credentials of a sympathiser' JC, 1980, 0 7145 3765 9, PB , 0 7145 3799 3, HC, D, pp. 98

Barker, Howard, 'stripwell' &'claw', JC, 1977, 0 7145 3566 4, HC, 0 7145 3572 9, PB, D, pp. 230

Barker, Howard, Seven Lears/Golgo, JC, 1990, 0 7145 4183 4, PB, D, pp. 81

Barker, Howard, 'the power of the dog' , JC 1985, 0 7145 4066 8 PB, D, pp. 44

Barker, Howard, The Possibilities, JC 1987, 0 7145 4135 4 PB, D, pp. 71

Barker, Howard, 'a passion in six days' :/ 'downchild' JC, 1985, 0 7145 3985

6, PB, D, pp. 108

Barker, Howard, 'women beware women'/'pity in history', JC, 1989, 0 7145 4134 6, PB, D, pp. 92

Barker, Howard, Women Beware Women, JC, 1986, 0 7145 4087 0, PB, D, pp. 36

Barker, Howard, Victory,/ Choices in Reaction, JC, 1983, 0 7145 3986 4, PB, D, pp.63

Ibsen, Henrik, An Enemy of the People, adapted by Stan Barstow, JC, 1978, 0 7145 3651 2, PB, D; pp. 58

Bataille, Georges, Eroticism, trans. Mary Dalwood, JC, 1962, ----------PB,--------- HC, E , pp. 276

Bataille, Georges, Literature and Evil, trans. Alastair Hamilton C&B, 1973, 0 7145 0345 2, HC, 0 7145 0346, PB, E, pp. 180

Baudelaire, Charles and Gautier, Theophile, Hashish Wine Opium, trans. Maurice Stang, C & B, 1972, 0 7145 0874 8 PB, 0 7145 0873 X, HC, E, pp. 92

Bauer, Wolfgang, 'all change' & other plays, trans. Martin and Renata Esslin, Herb Greer, C&B, 1973, 0 7145 0946 9, PB, 0 7145 0945 0, HC, D, pp. 180

Bellocchio, Marco, China is Near, trans. Judith Green, C & B, 1969, 0 7145 0724 5 PB, 0 7145 0723 7, HC, D, pp. 160

Benmussa, Simone, Benmussa Directs/ Portrait of Dora by Helene Cixous, The Singular Life of Albert Nobbs by Simone Benmussa, JC 1979, 0 7145 3730 6 PB, 0 7145 3764 0 HC, D, pp. 122

Beauvoir, Simone de, The Marquis de Sade, trans. & edited Paul Dinnage, JC, 1962, ------------, PB

Bennett, Hal, Lord of Dark Places, C& B, 1970, 0 7145 0800 4 HC, F, pp. 285

Bergman, Ingmar, a film trilogy: through a glass darkly/the communicants (Winter Light):the silence, trans. Paul Britten Austin, C & B, 1967, --------- HC, ---------PB, D, pp. 143

Bergman, Ingmar, Scenes from a Marriage, trans. Alan Blair, C & B, 1974, 0 7145 1086 6, HC, 0 7145 1087 4, PB, D, pp. 200

Bergman, Ingmar, persona & shame, C & B, trans. Keith Bradfield, 1972, 0 7145 0756 3, HC, 0 7145 0757 1, PB, D pp. 191

Bergonzo, Jean Louis, The Spanish Inn, trans. Helen R. Lane, C & B, 1970, 0 7145 0535 8, HC, 0 7145 0536 6, PB, F, pp. 112

Berkoff, Steven, Gross Intrusion & Other Stories, JC, 1979, 0 7145 3685 7 HC, ----------PB, F, pp.117

Berkoff, Steven, East/Agamemnon/The Fall of the House of Usher, JC, 1977, 0 7145 3610 5 HC, 0 7145 3636 7 PB, D, pp. 138

Berkoff, Steven, 'decadence'/'greek', JC 1982, Second printing 1986, 0 7145 3954 6 PB, D, pp. 92

Bessie, Alvah, The un-Americans, JC, 1957, --------HC, ---------PB F, pp. 383

Bobrowski, Johannes, Levin's Mill; trans. Janet Cropper, C & B, 1970, 0 7145 00250 8, HC, 0 7145 00216, PB, F, pp. 230

Bichsel, Peter, Stories for Children, trans. Michael Hamburger, C & B, 1971, 0 7145 0688 5, HC, 0 7145 0689 3, PB, F, pp. 57

Bichsel, Peter, And Really Frau Blum Would Very Much Like to Meet the Milkman, trans. Michael Hamburger, C & B, 1968, --------------HC, F, pp. 88

Samizdat text, Nobody or The Disgospel Accoording to Maria Dementnaya and Nikto(A Samizdat text) trans. April FitzLyon, JC, 1975, 0 7145 0975 2 HC, 0 7145 3551 6, PB, F, pp. 128

Boll, Heinrich, The Clown, trans. Leila Vennewitz, C & B, 1972, 1974, 1977, 0 7145 0964 7, HC, 0 7145 0168 9 PB, F, pp. 247

Boll, Heinrich , Billiards at Half Past Nine, trans. Patrick Bowles, J, 1965,--------
---PB, C & B, 1976, 0 7145 0124 7 PB, F, pp.245

Boll Heinrich, Absent Without Leave and other stories, trans. Leila Vennewitz, C&B, 1972, 0 7145 0938 8 PB; F, pp. 393

Bond, Edward, 'early morning', C & B, 1968, --------------PB, second impression 1971, JC, 1977, 0 7145 0206 5, HC, 0 7145 0207 3, PB, D, pp. 124

Borchert, Wolfgang, The Sad Geraniums and other stories, trans. Keith Hamnett, C & B, 1974, 0 7145 0805 5, HC, F, pp. 88

Borchert, Wolfgang, The Man Outside, trans. David Porter, J, 1966, ---------PB, F, pp. 257

Borgen, Johan, The Red Mist, trans. Oliver Stallybrass, C & B, 1973, 0 71456 0896 9, HC, F, pp. 111

Borgen Johan, Lillelord, trans. Elizabeth Brown Moen and Ronald E. Peterson, JC, 1982, 0 7145 3692 X, HC, 0 7145 3879 5 PB, F, pp. 312

Borges, Jorge Luis, Fictions, trans. Grove Press 1962, J, 1965, -----------PB, C & B, 1974, 0 7145 0957 4 HC, JC, 1985, 0 7145 4083 8 PB, F, pp. 159

Born, Nicolas, The Deception, trans. Leila Vennewitz, JC, 1983, 0 7145 3975 9 HC, 0 7145 3976 7 PB, F, pp.238

Boucourechliev, André, Schumann, Trans Arthur Boyars, JC, 1959, --------, PB, MB, 192pp

Bourdon, Sylvia, Love is a Feast, trans. Barbara Wright, JC, 1977, 0 7145 3648 2 HC, M, pp. 159

Bourniquel, Camille, Chopin, Trans. Sinclair Ross, EB, 1960, MB, --------, PB, 192pp

Breé, Germaine, Camus and Sartre: Crisis and Commitment, C & B, 1974, 0 7145 1010 6 HC, LC, pp. 287

Brenton, Howard,/ Clark, Brian,/ Griffiths, Trevor,/ Hare, David,/ Poliakoff, Stephen,/ Stoddart, Hugh,/ Wilson, Snoo,/ Lay By, C & B, 1972, 0 7145 0928 0 HC, 0 7145 0929 9, PB, D, pp. 72

Breytenbach, Breyten, In Africa Even The Flies Are Happy,: Selected Poems, 1964-1977, trans. Denis Hirson, JC, 1978, 0 7145 3696 2 HC, 0 7145 3871 X PB, P, pp. 148

Broderick, John, An Apology for Roses; C&B 1973, 0 7145 0898 5 HC, F, pp. 229

Brodsky, Michael, Detour, JC, 1979, 0 7145 3726 8 HC, F, pp. 359

Brook, Peter, Royal Shakespeare Theatre Production, US, C & B, 1968, --------
------PB, --------------HC, D, pp. 214

Brown, Alan, A Wind Up The Willow, JC 1980, 0 7145 3808 6 HC, 0 7145 3734 9, PB, F, pp. 96

Brown Alan, 'wheelchair willie'/'brown ale with gertie'/ ' o'connor', JC 1977, 0 7145 3652 0 HC, 0 7145 3655 5 PB, D, pp. 221

Brown, Alan, Skoolplay, JC 1978, 0 7145 3672 5 PB, D pp. 32

Bryher, The Days of Mars: A Memoir, 1940-1946, C & B, 1972, 0 7145 0942 -HC, M, pp. 190

Storm, Theodor,/ Buchner, Georg / Keller, Gottfried, German Classics: Immensee/ Lenz/A Village Romeo and Juliet, trans. Ronald Taylor/ Michael Hamburger: Ronald Taylor, C & B, 1966, ------------PB, D, pp. 188

Burford, E.J., The Orrible Synne: A Look at London Lechery from Roman to Cromwellian Times, C & B 1973, 0 7145 0978 7 HC, H, pp. 256

Burns, Alan, Celebrations, C & B, 1967, -----------PB, -----------HC, F pp.116

Burns, Alan, Babel, C & B, 1969, 0 7145 0010 0 HC, 0 7145 0011 9 PB, F, pp. 159

Burns, Alan, Europe After the Rain, JC, 1965, -----------HC, -----------PB, F, pp. 128

Burns, Alan, Dreamerika! C&B 1972, 0 7145 0803 9 HC, F, pp. 135

Burns, Carol, The Narcissist, C & B 1967, ---------HC, F, pp. 155

Burroughs, William, Dead Fingers Talk, JC in association with Olympia Press 1963, -----------HC, F, pp. 215

Burroughs, William, The Naked Lunch, JC in association with Olympia Press, 1964, 1965 1965, -------------HC, C & B in association with Olympia Press, 1965, 1966, 1970 0 7145 0391 6 HC, F, pp. 251

Burroughs, William, The Naked Lunch: A New Edition containing the "Ugh" Correspondence, JC, 1982, 0 7145 3969 4 PB, F, pp. 309

Burroughs, William, The Soft Machine, C & B, 1968, -------------HC , 0 7145 0732 6 PB, F , pp; 187

Burroughs, William, The Ticket that Exploded, C & B, 1968, ------------HC, 0 7145 0733 4 PB, JC, 1985 Second Edition, 0 7145 4072 2 PB, F, pp. 217

Burroughs, William, Exterminator!, C & B, 1974, 0 7145 0986 8 HC, 0 7145 0987 6 PB, JC 1984, F, pp. 168

Burroughs, William, The Job: Topical Writings and Interviews, with Daniel Odier, JC 1984, 0 7145 4028 5 PB, F, pp. 224

Burroughs, William S. The Wild Boys: A Book of the Dead, C & B, 1972 0 7145 0893 4 HC, 0 7145 0894 2 PB, JC 1972, 0 7145 0894 2, PB, F, pp. 184

Burroughs, William S. Cities of the Red Night, JC 1981, 0 7145 3784 5 HC, 0 7145 3816 7 PB, F, pp. 332

Burroughs, William S. Port of Saints, JC 1983, 0 7145 3948 1 HC, 0 7145 4017 X PB, F, pp. 184

Burroughs, William S. The Adding Machine: Collected Essays, JC 1985 0 7145 4073 0 HC, 0 7145 4143 5 PB, F, pp. 201

Burroughs, William S., The Place of Dead Roads, JC 1984, 0 7145 4030 7 HC, 0 7145 4032 3 PB, F, pp. 306

Burroughs, William, S., The Last Words of Dutch Schultz: A Fiction in the form of a Film Script, JC, 1986, 0 7145 4029 3 PB, F, pp. 117

Burroughs, William S., Ah Pook is Here and other Texts: The Book of Breeething Electronic Revolution JC 1979, 0 7145 3683 0 HC, 0 7145 3859 0 PB, F, pp. 158

Burroughs, William S., and Gysin Brion, The Third Man, JC, 1979, 0 7145 3737 3, HC, 0 7145 3862 0, PB, F, pp. 194

Busch, Frederick, I Wanted A Year Without Fall, C&B, 1971, 0 7145 0728 8? HC, 0 7145 0729 6, PB, F, pp.156

Busch, Frederick, Breathing Trouble and Other Stories, C&B, 1973, 0 7145 0899 3, HC, F, pp. 193

Butor, Michel, Passing Time, trans. Jean Stewart, J, 1965, ---------, PB,F, pp.288

Buzzati, Dino, Catastrophe, trans. Judith Landry and Cynthia Jolie, C&B, 1965, HC, F, pp.140

C

Canetti, Elias, Kafka's Other Trial: The Letters to Felice, trans. Christopher Middleton, C&B, 1974, 0 7145 1097 1, HC, 0 7145 1136 6, PB, F, pp.121

Cary, Joyce, Herself Surprised, J, 1968, ------------, PB, F, pp.214

Casey, Juanita, The Horse of Selene, The Dolmen Press/C&B, 1971, 85105 187 1, HC, 0 7145 1056 4, PB, F, pp.175

Casey, Juanita, The Circus, The Dolmen Press/C&B, 1974, 0 7145 1051 3, HC, F, pp.154

Cecchi, Dario, Titian, trans. Nora Wydenbruck, JC, 1957, ---------, HC, B, pp.232

Céline, Louis-Ferdinand, Journey to the End of the Night, trans. Ralph Mannheim, JC, 1988, 0 7145 3800 0, HC, 0 7145 4139 7, PB, M, pp.448

Céline, Louis-Ferdinand, Death On Credit, trans. Ralph Mannheim, JC, 1989, 0 7145 4157 5, HC, 0 7145 4179 6, PB, F, pp.592

Chamisso, Adalbert von, Peter Schlemihl, trans. Leopold von Loewenstein-Wertheim, JC, 1957, C&B, 1970, 0 7145 0439 4, HC, 0 7145 0440 8, PB, F, pp.94

Chekhov, Anton, The Woman in the Case and Other Stories, trans. April FitzLyon and Kyril Zinovieff, S&C, 1953, JC, 1954, Second impression,--------, HC, pp.190

Chekhov, Anton, Wife for Sale, trans. David Tutaev, JC, 1959, --------, HC,--------,PB pp.75

Cixous, Helene, Angst, trans. Jo Levy, JC, 1985, 0 7145 3905 8, PB, F, pp.219

Cixous, Helene, The Exile of James Joyce, trans. Sally A.. J. Purcell, JC, 1976, 0 7145 3507 9, HC, B, pp.765

Cocteau, Jean, Two Screenplays: The Blood of A Poet:The Testament of Orpheus, trans. Carol Martin-Sperry, C&B, 1970, 0 7145 0579 X, HC, 0 7145 0580 3, PB, D, pp. 144

Conn, Stewart, The Aquarium: The Man in the Green Muffler & I didn't Always Live Here, JC, 1976, 0 7145 3524 9, HC, 0 7145 3560 5, PB, D, D, pp.166

Conn, Stewart, The Burning, C&B, 1973, 0 7145 0831 4, HC, 0 7145 0832 2, PB, D, pp.102

Conrad, Borys, My Father Joseph Conrad, C&B, 1970, 0 7145 0018 6, HC, 0 7145 0019 4, PB, B, pp.176

Copi, Plays Volume 1: Eva Peron/The Homosexual or the Difficulty of Sexpressing Oneself/The four Twins/Loretta Strong, trans. Anni Lee Taylor, JC, 1976, 0 7145 3529 X, HC, 0 7145 3563 X, PB, D, pp.128

Coste, Dider, Sink Your Teeth Into The Moon, trans. Anita Barrows, C&B, 1974, 0 7145 1045 9, HC, F, pp. 172

Cotterell, A.F., 'the nutters' & other plays, C&B, 1971, 0 7145 0834 9, PB,0 7145 0833 0, HC, D, pp. 132

Cousin, Gabriel, 'black opera' & 'the girl who barks like a dog' trans. Irving F. Lycett, C&B, 1970, --------, HC, 0 7145 0693 1, PB, D, pp.170

Creeley, Robert, The Island, JC, 1964, -------, PB, HC, F, pp.190

Creeley, Robert, a Sense of Measure, C&B, 1972, 0 7145 0911 6, HC, 0 7145 0912 4, PB, F, pp.120

Creeley, Robert, The Charm: Early and Uncollected Poems, C&B, 1971, 0 7145 0820 9, HC, 0 7145 0875 6, PB, P, pp.196

Creeley, Robert, Poems: 1950-1965, C&B, 1966, ------, HC, ---------, PB, P, pp.228

Creeley, Robert, The Gold Diggers and Other Stories, JC, 1965, --------,HC, F, pp. 160

Creeley; Robert, The Finger: Poems 1966-1969, C&B, 1970, 0 7145 0422 X, HC, 0 7145 0423 8, PB, P, pp.144

Cremer, Jan, I Jan Cremer, English Version by R.E. Wyngaard and, Alexander Trocchi, C&B, 1965,-------, HC, B, pp.335

Cronin, Anthony, Dead As Doornails: A Memoir, The Dolmen Press/C&B, 1976, 0 7145 1092 0, HC, M, pp.201

Curteis, Ian, 'long voyage out of war': a trilogy of television plays, C&B, 1971, 0 7145 0783 0, HC, 0 7145 0784 9, PB, D, pp. 258

D

Dahlberg, Edward, The Sorrows of Priapus, With Drawings by Ben Shahn, C&B, 1970, 0 7145 0669 9, HC, 0 7145 0670 2, PB, NF, pp.120

Dahlberg, Edward, The Carnal Myth: A Search Into Classical Sensuality, C&B, 1970, 0 7145 0694 X, HC, 0 7145 0695 8, PB, NF, pp.122

Daniel, Yuli, Prison Poems, trans. Daniel Burg and Arthur Boyars, C&B, 1971, 0 7145 0789 X, HC, 0 7145 0790 3, PB , P, pp. 80

Dashkov, Princess, The memoirs of Princess Dashkov, trans. and Edited Kyril FitzLyon, JC, 1958, ----, HC,PB, ----- M, pp.322

Davie, Elspeth, Providings, JC, 1965, ------,HC, 0 7145 0665 6, PB, F, 202pp

Davie, Elspeth, The Spark and Other Stories; C&B, Reissued, JC, 1984, 1968, ------, HC, 0 7145 0538 2, PB, F, pp.218

Davie, Elspeth, Creating a Scene; C&B, 1971, 0 7145 0730 X , HC, 0 7145 0731 8, PB, F, pp.160

Davys, Sarah, A Time & A Time: An Autobiography, C&B, 1971, 0 7145 0706 7, HC, B, pp. 160

Dery, Tibor, The Giant/Behind the Brick Wall/Love, Trans. Kathleen Szasz, JC, 1964, -------, HC, F, 140pp

Dery, Tibor, The Portuguese Princess and Other Stories, trans. Kathleen Szasz, C&B, 1966, --------, HC, 0 7145 0486 6, F, 224pp

Dickens, Charles, The Supernatural Stories of Charles Dickens, edited by Michael Hayes, JC, 1978, 0 7145 3678 4, HC, F, 160pp

Dodd, Martha, The Searching Light, JC, 1956, -------, HC, F, pp. 345

Dostoievsky, Fyodor, Summer Impressions, Kyril FitzLyon, JC, 1955, -----PB, -- ----, HC, F, 122pp

Douassot, Jean, La Gana, trans. Alex Trocchi, C&B, 1974, 0 7145 0327 4, HC, F, 560pp

Drieu, La Rochelle, Pierre, Will O'The Wisp, Trans. Martin Robinson, C&B, 1966, 0 7145 013 3, PB, F, 144pp

Drozdowski, Bohdan, Editor, Twentieth Century Polish Theatre, Trans. Catherine Itzen, JC, 1979, 0 7145 3738 1, HC, D, 250pp

Droste-Hulshoff, Annette von, The Jew's Beech, trans. Lionel and Doris Thomas, JC, 1958, C&B, 1967, ------, HC, ------, PB, F, 80pp.

Dubillard, Roland, 'the swallows', trans. Barbara Wright, C&B, 1969, ------, HC, 0 7145 0648 6, PB, D, 120pp

Dubillard, Roland, 'the house of bones' trans. Barbara Wright, C&B, 1971, 0 7145 0766 0, HC, 0 7145 0767 9, PB, D, 160pp

Duckworth, Colin, Steps to the High Garden, CP, 1992, 0 7145 4155 9, HC, 0 7145 4229 6, PB, F, 288pp

Duras, Marguerite, Hiroshima Mon Amour and Une Aussi Longue Abescence, Trans. Richard Seaver/Barbara Wright; C&B; 1966, ------, HC, D, 192pp

Duras, Marguerite, The Square, Trans. Sonia Pitt-Rivers and Irina Morduch; JC, 1959, J, 1959, F, 108pp

Duras, Marguerite; Ten-Thirty On A Summer Night, Trans. Anne Borrchardt, JC, 1962,------- HC, ---------, PB, F, 108pp

Duras, Marguerite, Three Plays/ The Square/Days in the Trees/The Viaducts of Seine-et-Oise, trans. Barbara Bray and Sonia Orwell, C & B, 1967, ---------HC, D, pp. 159

Duras, Marguerite, The Sailor From Gibraltar, Trans. Barbara Bray, C&B, 1966, ------, HC, F, pp. 318

Duras, Marguerite, The Little Horses of Tarquinia, Trans. Peter DuBerg, JC, 1960, ------, HC, -------, PB, F, pp. 214

Duras, Marguerite, Moderato Cantabile, Trans. Richard Seaver, C&B, 1966, Reprinted, JC, 1987, CP, 1997, ------, HC, 0 7145 0381 9, PB, F, 120 pp

Duras, Marguerite, The Square/Ten-Thirty on a Summer Night/The Afternoon of Monsieur Andesmas, JC, 1977, 0 7145 3601 6, HC, 0 7145 3602 4, PB, F, 288pp

Duras, Marguerite, 'suzanna andler' 'la musica' & 'l'amante anglaise', Trans. Barbara Bray, JC, 1975, 0 7145 3506 0, HC, 0 7145 3508 7, PB, D, 140pp

Duras, Marguerite, The Afternoon of Monsieur Andesmas, Trans. Anne Borchardt, The Rivers and Forests, Trans. Barbara Bray, JC, 1964, ------HC, ------PB, F/D, 128pp

Duras, Marguerite, Whole Days in the Trees & other Stories, Trans. Anita Barrows, JC, 1984, 0 7145 3854 X, PB, F, 158pp

Durgnat, Raymond, Eros in the Cinema, C&B, 1966, -------HC, -------, PB, 208pp

E

Edwards, Page Jr., The Mules That Angels Ride, C&B, 1973, 0 7145 0990 6, HC, 160pp

Eichendorff, Joseph von, Memoirs of a Good For Nothing, Trans. Ronald Taylor, C&B, 1966, -----HC, 0 7145 0373 8, PB, F, 128pp

Eglites, Andrejs, Gallows Over Europe: Poems, Trans. Robert Fearnley and Velta Snikere, JC, 1984, 0 7145 4025 0, P, 128pp

Elliott, John, Another Example of Indulgence, C&B, 1970, 0 7145 0049 6, HC, F, 144pp

Eluard, Paul, Selected Poems, Selected and Translated by Gilbert Bowen, JC, 1987, 0 7145 3995 3, P, 158pp

Enzensberger, Christian, SMUT An Anatomy of Dirt, Trans. Sandra Morris, C&B, 1972, 0 7145 0913 2, HC, 0 7145 0914 0, PB, NF, 128pp

Esslin, Martin, Antonin Artaud, JC, 1976, 0 7145 3605 9, HC, LC, 128pp
Eveling, Stanley, 'come and be killed' & 'dear janet rosenberg, dear mr. Kooning' C&B, 1971, 0 7145 0749 0, HC, 0 7145 0750 4, PB, D, 150pp
Evans, Margiad, Autobiography, C&B, 1974, 0 7145 0977 9, HC, A, 192pp
Evans, Margiad, A Ray of darkness, JC, 1978, 0 7145 3727 6, HC, 0 7145 3607 5, PB, NF, 192pp
Evans, Margiad, Country Dance, Ill. Peggy Whistler, JC , 1978 07145 3593 1, HC, 07145 3728 4, PB, F, 96pp
Eveling, Stanley, 'the balachites' & 'the strange case of martin richter', C&B, 1970, 0 7145 0100 X, HC, 0 7145 0101 8, PB, D, 156pp
Eveling, Stanley, 'the lunatic, the secret sportsman and the woman next door' & 'vibrations', C&B, 1970, --------, HC, 0 7145 0701 6, D, 148pp
Ewen, Frederic, Bertolt Brecht: His Life, His Art and His Times, C&B, 1970, 0 7145 0120 4, HC, 0 7145 0121 2, PB, B, 574pp

F

Fairweather, Virginia, Cry God for Larry: An Intimate Memoir of Sir Laurence Olivier, C&B, 1969, 0 7145 0000 3, HC, B, 184pp
Farrell, James T., The Face of Time, S&C, 1954, ------, HC, F, 366pp
Fickelson, Maurice, Dod, Trans. J.A. Underwood, C&B, 1972, 0 7145 0810 1, HC, F, 192pp.
Figes, Eva, Tragedy and Social Evolution, JC, 1976 , 0 7145 3516 8, HC, 0 7145 3639 3, NF, 170pp
Fitzlyon, April, The Prince of Genius: A Life of Pauline Viardot, JC, 1964, -----,HC, 0 7145 0488 2, PB, B, 520pp
Fitzlyon, April, The Libertine Librettist: A Biography of Mozarts Librettist Lorenzo, da Ponte, JC, 1955, ------HC, B, 292pp
FitzLyon, April, Lorenzo da Ponte: A Biography of Mozart's Librettist, JC, 1982, PB, 0 7145 3783 7, PB, B, 292pp
Fletcher, John, Claude Simon and Fiction Now, C&B, 1975, 0 7145 1014 9, HC, 0 7145 1015 7, PB, LC, 240pp
Fletcher, John, New Directions in Literature, C&B, 1968, --------HC, -------, PB, LC, 176pp
Fletcher, John & Calder, John, Editors, The Nouveau Roman Reader, JC, 1986, 0 7145 3720 9, PB, F, 256pp
Foa, George R., The Blood Rushed to My Pockets, Ill. Michael Aryton, JC, 1957, -----, HC, F, 90pp
Forets, Louis-Rene des, The Children's Room, Trans. Jean SteWart, JC, 1963, ------, HC, 0 7145 0165 4, PB, F, 208pp
Foster, Paul, 'balls' & other plays, C&B, 1967, -------,HC, -----PB, D, 106pp
Foster, Paul, 'tom paine' C&B, 1967, ----HC, ---PB, D, 72pp
Foster, Paul, '!heimskringla!' or 'the stoned angels', C&B, 1970, 0 7145 0737 7, HC, 0 7145 0738 5, PB, D, 96pp
Foster, Paul, Marcus Brutus & Silver Queen Saloon, JC, 1977, 0 7145 3564 8, HC, 0 7145 3570 2, PB, D, 160pp
Foster, Paul, 'elizabeth I' & other plays, C&B, 1973, 0 7145 1028 9, HC, 0 7145 1029 7, PB, D, 174pp

Francis, André, Jazz, Trans. and Revised by Martin Williams, EB, 1960, --------, PB, MB, 189pp

Fried, Erich, Love Poems, Trans. Stuart Hood, CP, 1991, 0 7145 4185 0, PB, P, 330pp

Fried, Erich, 100 Poems Without A Country, Trans. Stuart Hood, JC, 1978, 0 7145 3694 6, HC, 0 7145 3884 1, PB, P, 148pp

Friel, George, The Boy Who Wanted Peace, JC, 1964, -----HC, -------PB, F, 232pp

Friel, George, Grâce and Miss Partridge, C&B, 1969, -----HC, 0 7145 0261 8, PB, F, 190pp

Friel, George, Mr. Alfred M.A., C&B, 1972, 0 7145 0770 9, HC, 0 7145 0771 7, PB, F, 218pp

Friel, George, An Empty House, C&B, 1974, 0 7145 0988 4, HC, F, 184pp

G

Gill, Peter, 'the sleeper's den' & 'over gardens out', C&B, 1970, 0 7145 0717 2, HC, 0 7145 0718 0, PB, P, 108pp

Gangemi, Kenneth, OLT, C&B, 1969, 0 7145 0659 1, HC, 0 7145 0660 5, PB, F, 64pp

Gallacher, Tom, 'mr. joyce is leaving paris' C&B, 1972, 0 7145 0924 8, HC, 0 7145 0925 6, PB, D, 96pp

Galloway, David, Melody Jones, JC, 1980, 0 7145 3807 8, HC, 0 7145 3733 0, PB, F, 120pp

Galloway, David, A Family Album, JC, 1978, 0 7145 3682 2, HC, 0 7145 3785 3, PB, F, 225pp

Galloway, David, Lamaar Ransom Private Eye, JC, 1979, 0 7145 3686 5, HC, F, 250pp

Gifford, Douglas, Editor, Scottish Short Stories 1800-1900, C&B, 1971, JC, 1981, 0 7145 0656 7, HC, 0 7145 0657 5, PB, F, 350pp

Goethe, Johann Wolfgang von, Selected Poems, Editor Christopher Middleton, JC, 1983, 0 7145 4004 8, PB, P, 298pp

Goethe, Johann Wolfgang von, The Sufferings of Young Werther, Trans. Bayard Quincy Morgan, JC, 1957, Reprinted, 1974, 1976, 0 7145 0541 2, HC, 0 7145 0542 0, PB, F, 160pp

Goethe, Johann Wolfgang von, Kindred by Choice, Trans. H.M. Waidson, JC, 1960, 1976, -----, HC, --------, PB, F, 290pp

Goethe, Johann Wolfgang von, Wilhelm Meister, Volume One, Trans. H.M. Waidson, JC, 1977, 0 7145 3675 X, HC, 0 7145 3924 4 , PB, F, 174pp

Goethe, Johann Wolfgang von, Wilhelm Meister, Volume Two, Trans. H.M. Waidson, JC, 1978, 0 7145 3699 7, HC, 0 7145 3926 0, PB, F, 185pp

Goethe, Johann Wolfgang von, Wilhelm Meister, Volume Three, Trans. H.M. Waidson, JC, 1979, 0 7145 3702 0, HC, 0 7145 3928 7, PB, F, 160pp

Goethe, Johann Wolfgang von, Wilhelm Meister, Volume Four, Trans. H.M. Waidson, JC, 1980, 0 7145 3827 2, HC, 0 7145 3930 9, PB, F, 128pp

Goethe, Johann Wolfgang von, Wilhelm Meister, Volume Five, Trans. H.M. Waidson, JC, 1981, 0 7145 3838 8, HC, 0 7145 3932 5, PB, F, 140pp

Goethe, Johann Wolfgang von, Wilhelm Meister, Volume Six, Trans. H.M. Waidson, JC, 1982, 0 7145 3840 X HC, 0 7145 3934 1, PB, F, 140pp

Gombrowicz, Witold, 'princess ivona', C&B, 1969, ------, PB, ------HC, D, 70pp

Gombrowicz, Witold, 'the marriage',Trans. Louis Iribarne, C&B, 1970, 0 7145 0645 1, HC, 0 7145 0646 X, PB, D, 152pp

Gombrowicz, Witold, Ferdydurke, Trans. Éric Mosbacher, C&B, 1965, ------PB, F, 272pp

Gombrowicz, Witold, Pornografia, Trans. Alastair Hamilton, C&B, 1966,-------- HC, 0 7145 0038 0, PB, F, 160pp

Gombrowicz, Witold, 'operetta' Trans. Louis Iribarne, C&B, 1971, 0 7145 0787 3, HC, 0 7145 0788 1, PB, D, 108pp

Gombrowicz, Witold, A Kind of Testament, Trans. Alastair Hamilton, Edited Dominique de Roux, C&B, 1973, 0 7145 0915 9, HC, M, 158pp

Gorz, Andre, The Traitor, Foreword Jean-Paul Sartre, Trans. Richard Howe, JC, 1960, -----, HC, -----, PB, F, 304pp

Gotthelf, Jeremias, The Black Spider, Trans. H.M. Waidson, JC, 1958, Reprinted 1965, 1980, 0 7145 0125 5, HC, 0 7145 0126 3, PB, F, 135pp

Goulet, Robert, Madhouse, C&B, 1973, 0 7145 1004 1, HC, 0 7145 1005 X, PB, F, 142pp

Griffiths, Trevor, 'occupations' & 'the big house', C&B, 1972, 0 7145 0880 2, HC, 0 7145 0881 0, PB, D, 134pp

Howard, Roger, 'slaughter night' & other plays, C&B, 1971, 0 7145 0841 1, HC, 0 7145 0842 X, PB, D, 92pp

Grimmelshausen, H.J.C. von, Simplicius Simplicissimus, Trans. Hellmuth Weissenborn and Lesley Macdonald, JC, 1964, -------HC, 0 7145 3910 4, PB, NF, 380pp

Gyllensten, Lars, The Testament of Cain, Trans. Keith Bradfield, C&B, 1967, ------, HC, F, 124pp

H

Hartenfels, Jerome, Lazarus, C&B, 1967, -------, HC, 0 7145 0335 5, PB, F, 307pp

Hartenfels, Jerome, Dr. Death, C&B, 1971, 0 7145 0686 9, HC, F, 232pp

Hauptmann, Gerhart, The Heretic of Soana, Trans. Bayard Quincy Morgan, JC, 1960, ----- HC, ----PB, F, 124pp

Hawthorne, Nathaniel, The Haunting Tales of Nathaniel Hawthorne, Edited Michael Hayes, JC, 1980, 0 7145 3809 4, HC, F, 162pp

Hayes, Michael, Editor, Supernatural Poetry: A Selection 16th Century to the 20th Century, JC, 1978, 0 7145 3677 6, HC, P, 190pp

Hedayat, Sadegh, The Blind Owl, Trans. D.P. Costello, Ill. Nancy Esdaile, JC, 1957, C&B, 1971, JC, 1986 ------HC, 0 7145 0133 6, PB, F, 134pp

Hennegan, J.M., Pulse, JC, 1977, 0 7145 3618 0, HC, 0 7145 3667 9, PB, F, 224pp

Heppenstall, Rayner, The Woodshed, J, 1968, -------,PB, F, 133pp

Heppenstall, Rayner, Raymond, Roussel: A Critical Guide, C&B, 1966, 0 7145 0048 8, PB, ------HC; LC, 98pp

Herburger, Gunter, A Monotonous Landscape, Trans. Goffery Skelton, C&B, 1969, 0 7145 0008 9, HC, 0 7145 0009 7, PB, F, 184pp

Higgins, Aidan, Images of Africa: Diary (1956-60) C&B, 1971, 0 7145 0774 1,

HC, 0 7145 0775 X, PB, M, 72pp

Higgins, Aidan, Felo De Se, JC, 1960, ------HC, ------PB, F, 190pp

Higgins, Aidan, Langrishe, Go Down, C&B, 1966, Reprinted 1972, JC, 1978, 0 7145 0328 2, HC, 0 7145 0329 0, PB, F, 272pp

Higgins, Aidan, Balcony of Europe, C&B, 1972, 0 7145 0102 6, HC, 0 7145 0103 4, PB, F, 464pp

Higgins, Aidan, Asylum and Other Stories, JC, 1960, Revised , JC; 1978, 0 7145 0229 4, HC, 0 7145 0230 8, PB, F, 192pp

Higgins, Aidan, Scenes From A Receeding Past, JC, 1977, 0 7145 3556 7, HC, 0 7145 3753 5, PB, F, 202pp

Himmelstrup, Kaj, 'welcome to dallas mr kennedy' Trans. Christine Hauch, C&B, 1971, 0 7145 0776 8, HC, 0 7145 0777 6, PB, D, 64pp

Hobson, Harold, Sir, French Theatre Since 1830, JC, 1978, 0 7145 3650 4, HC, 0 7145 3860 4, PB, LC, 262pp

Hoffmann, E.T.A., The Devil's Elixirs, Trans. Ronald Taylor, JC, 1963, -----,HC, -----, PB, M, 324pp

Hoffmann, E.T.A., The King's Bride, Trans. Paul Turner, JC, 1959, ---------, HC, F, 90pp

Howell, Anthony , Oslo: A Tantric Ode, C&B, 1975, 0 7145 1002 5, HC, P, 64pp

Hoyle, Trevor, The Man Who Travelled on Motorways, JC, 1979, 0 7145 3732 2, HC, 0 7145 3790 X, PB, F, 238pp

Hoyle, Trevor, Vail, JC, 1984, 0 7145 4055 2, PB, F, 190pp

Hoyle, Trevor, Blind Needle, CP, 1994, 0 7145 4252 0, F, 248pp

I

Imog, Jo, The Demon Flower, Trans. Catherine Hanf Noren, C&B, 1972, 0 7145 0811 X, HC, 0 7145 0812 8, PB, F, 220pp

Insingel, Mark, Reflections, Trans. Adrienne Dixon, C&B, 1971, 0 7145 0709 1, HC, 0 7145 0710 5, PB, F, 92pp

Ionesco, Eugene, Present Past Past Present: A Personal Memoir, Trans. Helen R. Lane, C&B, 1972, 0 7145 0909 4, HC, 0 7145 0910 8, PB, M, 192pp

Ionesco, Eugene, Notes and Counter-Notes, Trans. Donald Watson, JC, 1964, ---HC, 0 7145 0044 5, PB, NF, 280pp

Ionesco, Eugene, The Hermit, Trans. Richard Seaver, JC, 1983, 0 7145 3989 9, PB, F, 170pp

Ionesco, Eugene, Plays Volume 1, The Lesson, The Chairs, The Bald Prima Donna, Jacques or Obedience, Trans. Donald Watson, JC, 1958, 0 7145 0455 6, HC, JC, 1960, 1961, 1963, 1965, 1971, 1976, 0 7145 0456 4, PB, D, 150pp

Ionesco, Eugene, Plays Volume 2, Amedee, The New Tenant,Victims of Duty, Trans. Donald Watson, JC, 1958, JC, 1962, 1965, 1978, 0 7145 0457 2, HC, 0 7145 0458 0, PB, D, 166pp

Ionesco, Eugene, Plays Volume 3, The Killer, Improvisation, Maid to Marry, Trans. Donald Watson, JC, 1960, C&B, 1970, 0 7145 059 9, HC, 0 7145 0460 2, PB, D, 159pp

Ionesco, Eugene, Plays Volume 4, Rhinoceros, The Leader, The Future is in Eggs, Trans. Derek Prouse, JC, 1960, 1962, 1964, C&B, 1970, JC, 1978, ----HC, 0 7145 0462 9, D, 142pp

Ionesco, Eugene, Plays Volume 5, Exit the King, The Motor Show, Foursome, Trans. Donald Watson, JC, 1963, -----HC, C&B, 1970, 0 7145 0463 7, HC, 0 7145 0464 5, PB, D, 116pp

Ionesco, Eugene, Plays Volume 6, A Stroll in the Air, Frenzy for Two, Trans. Donald Watson, JC, 1965, C&B, 1970, 0 7145 0465 3, HC, 0 7145 0466 1, PB, D, 104pp

Ionesco, Eugene, Plays Volume 7, Hunger and Thirst, The Picture, Anger, Salutations, Trans. Donald Watson, C&B, 1968, 0 7145 0468 8, PB, D, 172pp

Ionesco, Eugene, Plays Volume 8, Here Comes A Chopper, The Oversight, The Foot of The Wall, Trans. Donald Watson, C&B, 1971, 0 7145 0760 1, HC, 0 7145 0761 X, PB, D, 136pp

Ionesco, Eugene, Plays Volume 9, Mackett, The Mire, Learning to Walk, Trans. Donald Watson, C&B, 1973, 0 7145 0959 0, HC, 0 7145 1052 1, PB, D, 166pp

Ionesco, Eugene, Plays Volume 10, Oh What A Bloody Circus, The Hard-boiled Egg, Trans. Donald Watson, JC, 1976, 0 7145 3510 9, HC, 0 7145 3515 X, PB, D, 134pp

Ionesco, Eugene, Plays, Volume 11, The Man With The Luggage, Trans. Donald Watson and Clifford Williams, The Duel, Double Act, Why Do I Write?, JC, 1979, 0 7145 3662 8, HC, 0 7145 3791 8, D, 135pp

Ionesco, Eugene, Plays, Volume 12, Journeys Among the Dead (Themes and Variations) Trans. Barbara Wright, JC, 1985, 0 7145 3956 2, PB, D, 65pp

Ionesco, Eugene, Plays, The Chairs, The Killer and Maid to Marry, JC, 1958, Reprinted 1960, J, 1963, D, 190pp

Irving, Washington, The Ghostly Tales of Washington Irving, Edited Michael Hayes, JC, 1979, 0 7145 3739 X, HC, F, 152pp

J

Jack, Ronald D.S., Editor, Scottish Prose 1550-1700, C&B, 1971, 0 7145 0798 9, HC, 0 7145 0799 7, PB, NF, 220pp

Jankelevitch, Vladimir, Ravel, Trans. by Margaret Crosland, JC, 1959, -------, PB, MB, 192pp

Janvier, Ludovic, The Bathing Girl, Trans. John Matthew, Revised Barbara Wright, JC, 1976, 0 7145 3519 2, HC, F, 112pp

Joans, Ted, A Black Manifesto in Jazz Poetry and Prose, C&B, 1971, 0 7145 0713 X, HC, 0 7145 0714 8, PB, NF/P, 94pp

Joans, Ted, A Black Pow-Wow of Jazz Poems, C&B, 1973, 0 7145 0903 5, HC, 0 7145 0904 3, PB, P, 160pp

Jones, Leroi, 'four black revolutionary plays', Experimental Death Unit 1, A Black Mass, Great Goodness of Life, Madheart, C&B, 1971, 0 7145 0843 8, HC, 0 7145 0844 6, PB, D, 72pp

Jodorowsky, Alexandro, El Topo: A Book of the Film, Trans. Joanne Pottlitzer, Edited Ross Firestone, C&B, 1974, 0 7145 1038 6, HC, 0 7145 1039 4, PB, D, 172pp

Jong, Dola de, The Tree and the Vine, Trans. Ilona Kinzer, JC, 1961, ------HC, ----PB, F, 128pp

Jupp, Kenneth, A Chelsea Trilogy, The Photographer; The Explorer, The Tycoon, C&B, 1969; 0 7145 0630 3, HC, 07145 0631 1, PB, D, 176pp

K

Kael, Pauline, Kiss Kiss Bang Bang, C&B, 1970, 0 7145 0658 3, HC, 0 7145 0983 3, PB, NF, 404pp

Kael, Pauline, Deeper Into Movies, C&B, 1975, 0 7145 0753 9,HC, 0 7145 0941 8, PB, NF, 458pp

Kafka, Franz, Letters to Friends, Family, Editors, Trans. Richard and Clara Winston, JC, 1978, 0 7145 3701 2, HC, NF, 508pp

Kaiser, Georg, Five Plays, From Morning to Midnight, The Burghers of Calais; The Coral, Gas I, Gas II, Trans. B.J. Kenworthy, Rex Last and J.N. Ritchie, C&B, 1971, JC, 1985, 0 7145 0241 3, HC, 0 7145 0242 1 PB, D, 272pp

Kaiser, Georg, Plays Volume Two, The Flight to Venice, One Day in October, The Raft of the Medusa, David and Goliath, The President, Trans. B.J. Kenworthy, H.F. Garton, Elizabeth Sprigge, JC, 1981, 0 7145 3763 2, HC, 0 7145 3899 X, PB, D, 205pp

Kavanagh, P.J., Only By Mistake, JC, 1986, 0 7145 4084 6, HC, 0 7145 4085 4, PB, F, 158pp

Kavanagh; P.J., People and Weather, JC, 1978, 0 7145 3666 0, HC, 0 7145 3666 0, PB, F, 170pp

Kaye, David, The Demise of A Poet, C&B, 1973, 0 7145 0969 8, HC, F, 138pp

Kaye David, The Australian, C&B, 1970, 0 7145 0095 X, HC, 0 7145 0096 8, PB, F, 175pp

Keller, Gottfried, Martin Salander, Trans. Kenneth Halwas, JC, 1964, ------HC, -------PB, F, 272pp

Keller, Gottfried, A Village Romeo and Juilette, Trans. Paul Bernard Thomas, JC, 1955, -------HC, F, 96pp

Keller, Gottfried, Green Henry, Trans. A.M. Holt, JC, 1960, JC, 1985, ----HC, 0 7145 0265 0, PB, F, 706pp

Kelly, Robert, The Scorpions, C&B, 1969, 0 7145 0516 1, HC, F, 188pp

Kennedy, R.C., The Golden Ass: A Version, JC, 1964, ----HC, F, 247pp

Kennedy, R.C., Annabelle Fast, C&B, 1966, Reissued from the original publication; The Golden Ass, 1964, ----PB, F, 247pp

Kershaw, Alister, A History of the Guillotine, JC, 1958, -----HC, ----, PB , H, 148pp

Kesey, Ken, One Flew Over the Cuckoo's Nest, C&B, 1972, Reprinted 1976, 1977, 0 7145 0871 3, HC, F, 255pp

Key-Aberg, Sandro, 'o' & 'an empty room' Trans. Brian Rothwell and Ruth Link, C&B, 1970, 0 7145 0735 0, HC, 0 7145 0736 9, PB, D, 144pp

Knowlson, James and Pilling John, Frescoes of the Skull: The Latter Prose and Drama of Samuel Beckett, JC, 1979, 07145 3643 1, HC, LC, 292pp

Koch, Stephen, Night Watch, C&B, 1970, 0 7145 0411 4, HC, F, 212pp

Koch, Stephen, Stargazer: Andy Warhol's World and His Films, C&B, 1973, 0 7145 1036 X, HC, 0 7145 1037 8, PB, NF, 155pp

Konstantinovic, Radomir, Exitus, Trans. E.D. Goy, C&B, 1965, ----HC, F, 252pp

Kureishi, Hanif, 'outskirts' 'the king and me' 'tommorow-today', JC, 1983,

0 7145 3971 6, D, 88pp
Kushchevsky, Ivan, Nikolai Negorev or the Successful Russian; Trans. D.P. and B. Costello, C&B, 1967, -----HC, 0 7145 0414 9, PB, F, 368pp

L

Lange, Monique, The Plane Trees, Trans. J.M. Calder, JC, 1961, --------, HC, ------, PB, F, 96pp
Lange, Monique, A Beach in Spain with Rue D'Aboukir & The Burial, Trans. J.A. Underwood, C&B, 1971, 0 7145 0109 3, HC, 0 7145 0110 7, PB, F, 105pp
Lavrin, Janko, Editor, an Anthology of Modern Ugoslav Poetry in English Translations, JC, 1962, -----PB, P, 199pp
Lawrence, Lars, Morning Noon and Night, JC, 1956, Second Impression, 1958, -----HC, F, 340pp
Lawrence; Lars, Old Father Antic, JC, 1961, -------HC, --------, PB, F, 460pp
Lawrence, Lars, The Hoax; JC, 1961, --------, HC, -------, PB, F, 367pp
Leale, B.C., The Colours of Ancient Dreams, JC, 1984, 0 7145 4037 4, PB, P, 96pp
Lettau, Reinhard, Obstacles, Trans. Ursule Molinaro and Ellen Sutton, C&B, 1966, F, 190pp
Lettau, Reinhard, Enemies, Trans. Agnes Rook, C&B, 1973, 0 7145 0711 3, HC, F, 72pp
Lettau, Reinhard, 'breakfast in miami', Trans. Julie Prandi and Reinhard Lettau, JC, 1982, 0 7145 3834 5, PB, D, 48pp
Lewis ,Wyndham, Blasting & Bombardiering: An Autobiography 1914-1926, C&B, 1967, JC, 1982, Revised edition, --------HC, 0 7145 0130 1, PB, 336pp
Lewis, Wyndham, Monstre Gai, J, 1965, -------PB, F, 253pp
Lewis, Wyndham, Malign Fiesta, J, 1966, -------PB, F, 240pp
Lewis, Wyndham, Tarr, J, 1968, ----PB, F, 300pp
Nadal, Rafael, Martinez, Lorca's Republic, C&B in Association with Lyrebird Press, 1974, 0 7145 1059 9, HC, LC, 247pp
Lucie-Smith, Edward, Thinking About Art: Critical Essays, C&B, 1968, -------, HC,0 7145 0553 6, PB, NF, 237pp
Lucian, True History and Lucius or the Ass, Trans. Paul Turner, JC, 1958, ------HC, -----PB, F, 108pp
Lund, James, The Ultimate, JC, 1976, 0 7145 3595 8, HC, 0 7145 3596 6, PB, F, 252pp

M

MacCaig, Norman, and Scott Alexander, Editors, Contemporary Scottish Verse 1959-1969, C&B, 1970, 0 7145 0178 6, HC, 0 7145 0179 4, PB, P, 272pp
McCoy, Sarah, Album and Other Stories, JC, 1983, 0 7145 4023 4, PB, F, 156pp
McGinn, Matt, Fry the Little Fishes, C&B, 1975, 0 7145 0992 2, HC, F, 145pp
McGovern, James, Fraulein, JC, 195?, -------HC, F, 312pp
McGovern, James, No Ruined Castles, JC, 1958, -------HC, -------PB, F, 287pp
McLean, Allan Campbell, The Glass House, C&B, 1969, -------HC, F, 204pp
MacGregor, Stewart, The Sinner, C&B, 1973, 0 7145 0955 8, HC, F, 256pp

McLellan, Robert, Jamie the Saxt, Edited by Ian Campbell and Ronald D.S. Jack, C&B, 1970, 0 7145 0306 1, HC, 0 7145 0307 X, PB, D, 157pp

McLellan, Robert, 'the hypocrite', C&B, 1970, --------HC, 0 7145 0280 4, PB, D, 122pp

McLellan, Robert, Collected Plays Volume 1, Torwatletie, The Carlin Moth, The Changeling, Jamie the Saxt, The Flouers O'Edinburgh, JC, 1981, 0 7145 3818 3, D, 278pp

McMillian, Dougald, Transition: The History of a Literary Era 1927-1938, C&B, 1975, 0 7145 1016 5, HC, LC, 303pp

McMillian, Dougald, and Fehsenfeld Martha, Beckett in the Theatre, JC, 1988, 0 7145 3952 X, HC, LC, 333pp

Magalaner, Marvin, and Kain, Richard M., Joyce: The Man, The Work, The Reputation, JC, 1956, -----HC, LC, 377pp

Maillet, Antoine, Pelagie-la-Charrette, Trans. Phillip Stratford,JC, 1982, 0 7145 3945 7, HC, 0 7145 3966 X, PB, F, 250pp

Mallea, Eduardo, Chaves and Other Stories, Trans. Maria Mercedes Aspiazu, John B. Hughes, Helen B. MacMillan, Harriet de Onis, and Maria Angelica Deulofeu, C&B, 1970, 0 7145 0161 1, HC, 0 7145 0162 X, PB, F, 190pp

Mallea, Eduardo, All Green Shall Perish; Trans. John B. Hughes, C&B, 1967, -----,HC, -------PB, F, 158pp

Mallea, Eduardo, Fiesta in November, Trans. Alis de Sola, C&B, 1968, -------HC, 0 7145 0003 8, PB, F, 121pp

Mallin, Tom, 'curtains' C&B, 1971, 0 7145 0792 X, HC, 0 7145 0793 8, PB, D, 106pp

Maltz, Albert, A Long Day in A Short Life, JC, 1957, ------HC, -------, PB, F, 320pp

Maltz, Albert, A Tale of One January, C&B, 1966, ------ HC, 0 7145 0544 7, PB, F, 158pp

Mandiargues, Andre Pieyre de, The Girl Beneath the Lion, Trans. Richard Howard, JC, 1959, --------- HC, -------PB, J, 1963, PB, -------, F, 144pp

Mandiargues, Andre Pieyre de, The Margin, Trans. Richard Howard, C&B, 1969, 0 7145 0362 2, HC, 0 7145 0363 0, PB, F, 216pp

Mandiargues, Andre Pieyre de, Blaze of Embers, Trans. April FitzLyon, C&B, 1971, 07145 0131 X, HC, 0 7145 0132 8, PB, F, 128pp

Mandiargues, Andre Pieyre de, The Girl on the Motorcycle, Trans. Alexander Trocchi, C&B, 1966, -------HC, -------PB, F, 164pp

Manet, Eduardo, 'the nuns' Trans. Robert Baldick, C&B, 1970, 0 7145 0721 0, HC, 0 7145 0722 9, PB, D, 92pp

Maquet, Albert, Albert Camus: The Invincible Summer, JC, 1958, -------, HC,LC, 224pp

Marceau, Félicen, Creezy, Trans. J.A. Underwood, C&B, 1970, 0 7145 0708 3, HC, F, 122pp

Marowitz, Charles, 'a macbeth', C&B, 1971, 0 7145 0719 9, HC, 0 7145 0720 2, PB, D, 106pp

Marowitz, Charles, 'the shrew', C&B, 1975, 0 7145 1118 8, HC, -------, PB, D, 80pp

Matthews, W.K. and Slodnjak, A., editors, The Parnassus of a small Nation: An Anthology of Slovine Lyrics, JC, 1957, ----, HC, P, 140pp

Matura, Mustapha, 'as time goes by' & 'black pieces', C&B, 1972, 0 7145 0822

9, HC, 0 7145 0883 7, PB, D, 144pp

Mauriac, Claude, Femmes Fatales, Trans. Henry Wolff; C&B, 1966, ------, HC, 0 7145 0232 4, F, 228pp

Mauriac, Claude, Dinner in Town, Trans., Merloyd Lawrence, JC, 1963, -----, HC, ------, PB, F, 320pp

Mauriac, Claude, The Marquise Went Out At Five, Trans. Richard Howard, C&B, 1966, -----, HC, 0 7145 0367 3, PB, F, 312pp

May, Naomi, At Home, C&B, 1969, ----, HC, 0 7145 0094 1, PB, F, 186pp

May, Naomi, The Adventurer, C&B, 1970, 0 7145 0697 4, HC, F, 191pp

May, Naomi, Troubles, JC, 1976, 0 7145 3555 9, HC, 0 7145 3606 7 PB, F, 248pp

Mechanicus, Philip, Waiting For Death, Trans. Irene R. Gibbons, C&B, 1964, ----HC, M, 267pp

Melhem, D.H., Blight, CP, 1994, 0 7145 4274 1, HC, F, 145pp

Mendel, R.W.S., Revelation in Shakespeare, JC, 1964, -----, HC, ----, PB, LC, 224pp

Mercer, David, The Generations: A Trilogy of Plays, Where the Difference Begins, A Climate of Fear and The Birth of A Private Man, JC, 1964, -----, HC, ----PB, D, 282pp

Mercer, David, 3 TV Plays: A Suitable Case for Treatment, For Tea on Sunday, And Did Those Feet, C&B, 1966, ------, HC, ------, PB, D, 140pp

Mercer, David, Belcher's Luck, C&B, 1967, -------HC, -------, PB, D, 110pp

Mercer, David, Ride a Cock Horse, C&B, 1966, ----HC, -----PB, D, 94pp

Mercer, David, Collected TV Plays: 1, Where the Difference Begins, A Climate of Fear, The Birth of a Private Man, JC, 1981, (originally published as The Generations: A Trilogy of Plays JC, 1964), 0 7145 3722 5, HC, 0 7145 3723 3, PB, D, 282pp

Mercer, David, Collected TV Plays: 2, A Suitable Case for Treatment, For Tea on Sunday, And Did Those Feet, The Parachute, Let's Murder Vivaldi, In Two Minds, JC, 1981, 0 7145 3814 0, HC, 0 7145 3817 5, PB, D, 290pp

Mercer, David, The Parachute, C&B, 1967, ------, HC, ----PB, D, 156pp

Mérimée, Prosper, A Slight Misunderstanding, Trans. ˜Douglas Parmée, JC, 1959, -----, HC, -----, PB, F, 104pp

Merle, Iris, Portugese Panorama, JC, 1959, -----PB, NF, 224pp

Michaux, Henri, Infinite Turbulence, Trans. Michael Fineberg, C&B, 1975, 0 7145 1018 1, HC, NF, 190pp

Miller, Henry, Tropic of Cancer, JC, 1963, ----, HC, F, 318pp

Miller, Henry, Tropic of Capricorn, JC, 1964, ----, HC, F, 316pp

Miller, Henry, Black Spring, JC, 1965, ----- HC, J, 1968, --------PB, F, 201pp

Miller; Henry, Sexus, C&B, 1969, Reprinted, 1971, 0 7145 0525 0, HC, F, 506pp

Miller, Henry, Quiet Days in Clichy, C&B, 1966, -----, HC, F, 124pp

Miller, Henry, The World of Sex & Max and the White Phagocytes, C&B, 1970, 0 7145 0617 6, HC, -----PB, F, 126pp

Miller, Henry, Sextet: Six Essays, JC, 1980, 0 7145 3828 0, HC, 0 7145 3844 2, PB, NF, 188pp

Miller, Henry, The World of Lawrence: A Passionate Appreciation, JC, 1985, CP, 1993, 0 7145 3867 1, PB, 0 7145 3866 3, HC, NF, 272pp

Morike, Eduard, Mozart's Journey to Prague, Trans. Leopold von Loewenstein-Wertheim, JC, 1957, Reprinted 1964, 1976, 1985, 0 7145 0388 6, HC, 0 7145 0389 4, PB, NF, 93pp

Morin, Edgar, The Stars, Trans. Richard Howard, JC, 1960, ------, PB, NF, 192pp

Moor, George, Fox Gold Nightingale Island Bowl of Roses, JC, 1978, 0 7145 3615 6, HC, F, 176pp

Morris, Edita, Love to Vietnam, C&B, 1969, ----HC, ------, PB, F, 92pp

Motte Fouqué, F.H.K. de la, Undine, Trans. Paul Turner, JC, 1960, ---HC, ---PB, F, 128pp

Mowat, David, 'anna-luse' & other plays, C&B, 1970 0 7145 0643 5, HC 0 7145 0644 3, PB, D, 192pp

Mowat, David, 'the others', C&B, 1973, 0 7145 0845 4, HC, 0 7145 0846 2, PB, D, 118pp

Mulisch, Harry, Two Women, Trans. Els Early, JC, 1980, 0 7145 3810 8, HC, 0 7145 3839 6, PB, F, 126pp

N

Nance, William, L., The Worlds of Truman Capote, C&B, 1973, 0 7145 0920 5, HC, LC, 256pp

Navarre, Yves, Sweet Tooth, Trans. Donald Watson, JC, 1976, 0 7145 3522 2, HC, F, 220pp

Navarre, Yves, Cronus' Children, Trans. Howard Girven, JC, 1986, 0 7145 4013 7, HC, 0 7145 4014 5, PB, F, 320pp

Nemec, David, The Systems of M.R. Shurnas, JC, 1985, 0 7145 4022 6, PB, F, 126pp

Newman, Charles, New Axix or The "Little Ed" stories, C&B, 1968, -------HC, 0 7145 0074 7, PB, F, 128pp

New Writers 1: Monique Lange, Alan Burns, Dino Buzzati 1961, -------, HC, ------, PB, F, 188pp

New Writers 2: Simon Vestdijk, Miodrag Bulatovic, Keith Johnstone, Robert Pinget/English Adaptation by Samuel Beckett, JC, 1962, -------HC, -------PB, L, 127pp

New Writers 3: Alexander Trocchi, Nick Rawson, Sinclair Beiles, David Mercer, JC, 1965, ------PB, ------HC, L, 132pp

New Writers 4: Plays and Happenings; Jean-Jacques Label, E.C. Nimmo, Charles Marowitz, Ken Dewey, René de Obaldia, Allan Kaprow, John Antrobus, C&B, 1967, -----HC, ----PB, L, 166pp

New Writers : Daniel Castelain, Alex Neish, Nazli Nour, C&B, 1966, ----HC, ----PB, L, 190pp

New Writers 6: Carol Burns, Penelope Shuttle, J.A. Dooley, C&B, 1967, ------ HC, ----PB, L, 224pp

New Writers 7: Tina Morris, Edmund Crackenedge, Kanwal Sundar, 0 7145 0012 7, HC, 0 7145 0013 5, PB, L, 190pp

New Writers 8: Christine Bowler, Lyman Andrews, F.W. Willetts, C&B, 1968, 0 7145 0014 3, HC, 0 7145 0015 1, PB, L, 180pp

New Writers 9: Renata Rasp, Amanda Smyth, John Donovan, C&B, 1971, 0 7145 0016 X, HC, 0 7145 0017 8, PB, L, 144pp

New Writers 10: Floyd Salas, Gerald Robitaille, Earl Coleman, C&B, 1971,0 7145 0751 2, HC, 0 7145 0752 0, PB, L, 224pp

New Writers 11: Svend Age Madesen, David Mowat, J.M. Hennegan, 0 7145 0813 6, HC, 0 7145 0814 4, PB, L, 224pp

New Writers 12: David Galloway, Patrick Morrissey, Joyce Mansour, JC, 1976, 0 7145 3542 7, HC, 0 7145 3545 1, PB, L, 224pp

New Writing and Writers 13: Samuel Beckett, Steven Berkoff, Nikolai Bokov, Edward Bond, Elspeth Davie, Tony Duvert, A.R. Lamb, Gertrude Leutenegger, Naomi May, George Moor, N.E. Nikto, Antonia Pozzi, Roderick Watson, JC, 1976, 0 7145 3552 4, hC, 0 7145 3541 9, PB, L, 224pp

New Writing and Writers 14: Ingeborg Bachmann, Ann Benedek, Nikolai Bokov, Edward Bond, Pierre Bourgeade, Dino Buzzati, Peter French, Sadegh Hedayat, P.J. Kavanagh, René de Obaldia, Peter-Paul Zahl, JC, 1978, 0 7145 3562 1, HC, 0 7145 3553 2, PB, L, 220pp

New Writing and Writers 15: Heinrich Boll, Alan Brown, Micheal Horovitz, P.J. Kavanagh, Jessie Kesson, JC, 1978 0 7145 3554 0, HC, 0 7145 3561 3, PB, L, 350pp

New Writing and Writers 16: William Burroughs, Dino Buzzati, David Craig, Elspeth Davie, Ingeborg Drewitz, Kathleen Greenwood, Maryon Jeane, Neil Jordan, Sarah Lawson, B.C. Leale, Sarah McCoy, Michael Moorcock, JC, 1979, 0 7145 3635 0, HC, 0 7145 3638 5, PB, L, 192pp

New Writing and Writers 17: Samuel Beckett, Nikolai Bokov, Jan Cremer, Harry Mulisch, Yves Navarre, Robert Pinget, John Wynne, JC, 1980 0 7145 3693 8, HC, 0 7145 3695 4, PB, L, 302pp

New Writing and Writers 18: Yves Bonnfoy, Copi, A.R. Lamb, B.C. Leale, Harry Mulisch, Naiwu Osahon, Calum Ross, Tibor Varady, JC, 1980, 0 7145 3773 X, HC, 0 7145 3774 8, PB, L, 244pp

New Writing and Writers 19: Edward Bond, Copi, Patrick Morrissey, Harry Mulisch, Martin Walser, Kenneth White, JC, 1982, 0 7145 3815 9, HC, 0 7145 3811 6, PB, L, 262pp

New Writing and Writers 20: Samuel Beckett, Nikolai Bokov, Pat Connoly, Sorel Etrog, George Moor, JC, 1983, 0 7145 3869 8, PB, L, 188pp

Nuttall, Jeff, Performance Art: Memoirs, JC, 1979, 0 7145 3711 X, HC, 0 7145 3788 8, PB, M, 190pp

Nuttall, Jeff, Snipe's Spinster, C&B, 1975, 0 7145 1089 0, HC, 0 7145 1090 4, PB, F, 118pp

Nye, Robert, Darker Ends, C&B, 1969, 0 7145 0185 9, HC, 0 7145 0186 7, PB, P, 64pp

Nye, Robert, & Watson Bill, 'sawney bean', C&B, 1970, -----, HC, 0 7145 0691 5, PB, D, 108pp

Nye, Robert, Tales I Told My Mother, C&B, 1969, 0 7145 0022 4, HC, 0 7145 0023 2, PB, F, 172pp

Nye, Robert, Doubtfire, C&B, 1967, ----, HC, 0 7145 0201 4, PB, F, 208pp

O

Obaldia, Rene de, The Centenarian, Trans. Alexander Trocchi, C&B, 1970, 0 7145 0159 X, HC, 0 7145 0160 3, PB, F, 192pp

Obaldia, Rene de, Plays volume 1: Genusia, Seven Impromptus for Leisure, Trans. Donald Watson, C&B, 1965, ----HC, 0 7145 0470 X, PB, D, 192pp

Obaldia, Rene de, Plays Voume 2, The Satyr of La Villette, The Unknown General, Wide Open Spaces, Trans. Donald Watson, C&B, 1970, 0 7145 0471 8, HC, 0 7145 0472 6, PB, D, 173pp

Obaldia, Rene de, Plays Volume 3: Two Women for one Ghost, The Baby-Sitter, The Jellyfishes' Banquet, Trans. Donald Watson, JC, 1982, 0 7145 3559 1,PB, D, 80pp

Obaldia, Rene de, Plays Volume 4, Monsieur Klebs and Rozalie, Wind in The Branches of the Sassafras, Trans. Barbara Wright and Joseph Foster, JC, 1985, 0 7145 3664 4, PB, D, 104pp

Obaldia, Rene de, 'wind in the branches of the sassafras', Trans. Joseph Foster, C&B, 1969, --------PB, -----HC, D, 108pp

O'Brien, Fitz-James, The Fantastic Tales of Fitz-James O'Brien, Editor Michael Hayes, JC, 1977; 0 7145 3617 2, HC, F, 150pp

O'Brien, Tim, If I Die In A Combat Zone, C&B, 1973, 0 7145 1006 8, HC, F, 199pp

O'Casey, Sean, Niall: A Lament, CP, 1991, 0 7145 4196 6, HC, M, 96pp

Orlovitz, Gil, Milkbottle H, C&B, 1967, --------HC, --------PB, F, 534pp

Orlovitz, Gil, Ice Never F, C&B, 1970, 0 7145 0281 2, HC, 0 7145 0282 0, PB, F, 333pp

Osborne, Charles, Letter to W.H. Auden and Other Poems, 1941-1984, JC, 1984, 0 7145 4036 6, PB, P, 96pp

Ovid, The Art of Love, Trans. Rolfe Humphries, JC, 1958, ------HC, P, 206pp

Ovid, Metamorphoses, Trans. Rolfe Humphries, JC, 1957, --------HC,L, 401pp

P

Pasolini, Pierre-Paolo, Selected Poems, Trans. Norman MacAfee qnd Luciano Martinengo, JC, 1984, 0 7145 3889 2, PB, P, 231pp

Paz, Octavio, An Anthology of Mexican Poetry, Trans. Samuel Beckett; C&B, 1970, 0 7145 0086 0 PB, P, 213pp

Pedretti, Erica, Stones, Trans. Judith L. Black, JC, 1982, 0 7145 3929 5, HC, F, 186pp

Penrose, Valentine, The Bloody Countess Trans. Alexander Trocchi, C&B, 1970, 0 7145 0134 4, HC, (Released as Countess Dracula, PB,)0 7145 0135 2, PB, F, 192pp

Petronius, Satryricon, Trans. Paul Dinnage, S&C, 1953, -----HC, L, 162pp

Pharr, Robert Deane, The Book of Numbers, C&B, 1970, 0 7145 0696 6, HC, F, 374pp

Picasso, Pablo, 'desire caught by the tail', Trans. Sir Ronald Penrose, C&B, 1970, 0 7145 0190 5, HC,7145 0191 3, PB, D, 64pp

Picasso, Pablo, 'the four little girls' trans. Sir Ronald Penrose, C&B, 1970, 0 7145 0637 0, HC, 0 7145 0638 9, PB, D, 96pp

Pinget, Robert, No Answer, Trans. Richard N. Coe, JC, 1961, -----HC, ------PB, F, 151pp

Pinget, Robert, Fable, Trans. Barbara Wright, JC, 1980, 0 7145 3792 6, HC, 0 7145 3792 6, PB, F, 58pp

Pinget, Robert, Recurrent Melody (Passacaille) Trans. Barbara Wright, C&B, 1975, 0 7145 1088 2, HC, F, 96pp

Pinget, Robert, The Libera Me Domine, Trans. Barbara Wright, C&B, 1972, 0 7145 0339 8, HC, 0 7145 0340 1PB, F, 215pp

Pinget, Robert, Baga, Trans. John Stevenson, C&B, 1967, -----HC, 0 7145 0099 2, PB, F, 135pp

Pinget, Robert, The Inquisitory, Trans. Donald Watson, C&B, 1966, ----HC, 0 7145 3911 2, F, 400pp

Pinget, Robert, MAHU or The Material, Trans. Alan Sheridan-Smith, C&B, 1966, ----HC, 0 7145 0354 1, PB, F, 144pp

Pinget, Robert, Plays Volume 1 Dead Letter, The Old Tune (English Adaptation by Samuel Beckett), Clope, Trans. Barbara Bray, JC, 1963, -----HC, ---PB, D, 132pp

Pinget, Robert, Plays Volume 2, Architruc, About Mortin, The Hypothesis, Trans. Barbara Bray, C&B, 1967, -----HC, 0 7145 0038 0, PB, D, 192pp

Pirandello, Luigi, Collected Plays, Volume One, Henry IV, The Man With the Flower in His Mouth, Right You Are (If You Think You Are), Lazarus, JC, 1987, Reprinted, 1998, 0 7145 4110 9, PB, D, 224pp

Pirandello, Luigi, Collected Plays Volume Two, Six Characters in Search of an Author, All for the Best, Clothe the Naked, Limes From Sicily, JC, 1988, Reprinted 1998, 0 7145 3984 8, PB, D, 232pp

Pirandello, Luigi, Collected Plays Volume Three, The Rules of the Game, Each in his Own Way, Grafted, The Other Son, CP, 1992, 0 7145 4181 8, PB, D, 202pp

Pirandello, Luigi, Volume Four, As You Desire Me, Think it Over, Giacomino! This Time it Will Be Different, The Imbecille, CP, 1996, 0 7145 4271 7, PB, D, 252pp

Pollini, Francis, Night, JC,(In Association with Olympia Press), 1961, -----, HC, ---PB, F, 250pp

Pozzi, Antonia, Poems, Trans. Nora Wydenbruck, JC, 1955, ----HC, P, 231pp

Q

Quackenbush, Jan, 'inside out' & other plays, C&B, 1968, ----HC, -----, PB D, 72pp

Quackenbush, Jan, 'calcium & other plays, C&B, 1971, 0 7145 0849 7, HC, 0 7145 0850 PB, D, 92pp

Queneau, Raymond, Exercizes in Style, Trans. Barbara Wright, JC, 1979, Reprinted 1981, 1998, 0 7145 3750 0, HC, 0 7145 4238 5, PB, F, 197pp

Queneau, Raymond, We Always Treat Women Too Well, Trans. Barbara Wright, JC, 1981, 0 7145 3687 3, HC, 0 7145 3736 5, PB, F, 174pp

Queneau, Raymond, Zazie In the Metro, Trans. Barbara Wright, JC, 1982, 0 7145 3872 8, HC, 0 7145 3923 6, PB, F, 208pp

Queneau, Raymond, The Bark-Tree, (Le Chiendent) Trans. Barbara Wright, C&B, 1968, -----HC, 0 7145 0108 5, PB, F, 284pp

Queneau, Raymond, The Sunday of Life Trans Barbara Wright, JC 1976, 0 7145 3521 4 HC 0 7145 3641 5 PB F 200 pp.

Queneau, Raymond, The Flight of Icarus trans. Barabara Wright C & B. 1973 0 7145 0963 9 HC 0 7145 1144 7 PB F 192 pp.

Quinn, Ann Berg, JC 1964 ----------------HC -----------PB F 168 pp;

Quinn, Ann, Three C & B 1966 ----------HC ---------PB F 144 pp;
Quinn, Ann, Passages C & B 1969 --------HC 0 7145 0056 9 PB F 112pp.

R

Raabe, Paul, The Era of German Expressionism, trans. J. M. Ritchie C & B 1974 0 7145 0698 2 HC, 0 7145 0699 0 PB NF 424 pp.
Radiguet, Raymond, Cheeks on Fire: Collected Poems trans. Alan Stone JC 1976 0 7145 3513 3 HC 0 7145 3575N 3 PB 113 pp.
Radiguet, Raymond, The Devil in the Flesh trans. A. M. Sheridan Smith C & B 1968 --------------HC -----------PB 128 pp.
Radiguet, Raymond, Count D'Orgel trans. Violet Schiff Preface Jean Cocoteau J/C & B 1968 ----------HC 0 7145 0813 2 PB 214 pp.
Rasp, Renate, A Family Failure trans. Eva Figes C & B 1970 0 7145 0668 0 HC 0 7145 0707 5 PB 126 pp.Rawson, Nicholas, Shards C & B 1973 0 7145 0754 7 HC P 180 pp.
Reavey, George, editor and translator, The New Russian Poets: 1953-68; Bilingual Edition C & B 1968 --------HC P 282 pp.
Reissner, Alexander, Return to Katja JC 1958 ---------HC F 132 pp.
Reissner, Alexander The Belfry of Bruges JC 1962 ---------HC --------PB F 48 pp.
Resnick, Seymour and Pasmantier, Jeanne, Editors, An Anthology of Spanish Literature in English Translation JC 1958 ----------HC P 608 pp.
Riddell, Alan, Eclipse: Concrete Poems 1963-1971 C & B 1972 P 64 pp. 0 7145 0907 8 HC 0 7145 0908 6 PB
Ribnikar, Jara, I & You & She, trans. Eva Tucker C & B 1972 0 7145 0815 2 HC 0 7145 0885 3 PB F 208 pp.
Ritchie, J. M., Editor, Seven Expressionist Plays: Kokoschka to Barlach trans. J.M.Ritchie and H.F.Garten C & B 1968 JC 1980 --------HC 0 7145 0521 8 PB D 202pp.
Ritchie, J.M. Editor, Vision and Aftermath: Four Expresssionist War Plays, trans. J.M.Ritchie and J.D.Stowell C & B 1968 -------HC 0 7145 0599 4 PB D 208 pp.
Ritchie, Paul , The Protagonist C & B 1966 -------HC -------PB F 219 pp.
Ritchie, Paul, Confessions of a People Lover C & B 1967 --------HC F 158 pp.
Ritchie, Paul, 'saint honey' & 'oh david, are you there?' C & B 1968 ------HC -------PB D 124 pp.
Roché, Henri-Pierre, Jules and Jim trans. Patrick Evans JC 1963 -----------HC F 240 pp.
Robbe-Grillet, Alain, The Erasers Trans. Richard Howard C & B 1966 JC 1987-------HC 0 7145 0214 6 PB F 220 pp.
Robbe-Grillet, The Voyeur, Trans Richard Howard JC 1959 reprinted 1965, 1971 JC 1980,--------HC 0 7145 0601 X PB F 220 pp.
Robbe-Grillet, Alain, Jealousy, Trans. Richard Howard, JC, 1960, J, 1965, JC, 1977, JC, 1987, JC, 1997, ------HC, 0 7145 0311 8, PB, F, 104pp
Robbe-Grillet, Alain, In the Labyrinth, Trans. Christine Brooke-Rose, C&B, 1967, JC, 1980, -----HC, 0 7145 0298 7, PB, F, 189pp.
Robbe-Grillet, Alain, Last Year at Marienband: A cinè novel, Trans. Richard Howard, JC, 1962, ----HC, -----PB, F, 152pp

Robbe-Gillet, Alain, The Immortal One, A.M. Sheridan Smith, C&B, 1971, 0 7145 0286 3, HC, 0 7145 0287 1, PB, F, 174pp

Robbe-Grillet, Alain, The House of Assignation, Trans. A.M. Sheridan Smith, C&B, 1970, 0 7145 0275 8, HC, 0 7145 0276 6, PB, F, 124pp

Robbe-Grillet, Alain , Project for a Revolution in New York, Trans. Richard Howard, C&B, 1973, 0 7145 0956 6, HC, 0 7145 1071 8, PB, F, 183pp

Robbe-Grillet, Alain, Topology of a Phantom City, Trans. J.A. Underwood, JC, 1978, 0 7145 3632 6, HC, 0 7145 3740 3, PB, F, 142pp

Robbe-Grillet, Alain, Snapshots and Towards a New Novel, Trans. C&B, 1965, -----HC, 0 7145 0531 5, PB, F, 162pp

Robbe-Grillet, Alain, Ghosts in the Mirror, Trans. Jo Levy, JC, 1988, 0 7145 4093 5, HC, 0 7145 4094 3, PB, F, 160pp

Robbe Grillet, Alain, Recollections of the Golden Triangle, Trans. JJ.A. Underwood, JC, 1984, 0 7145 4026 9, PB, F, 157pp

Robbe-Grillet, Alain, Djinn, Trans. Yvonne Lenard and Walter Wells, JC, 1983, 0 7145 3978 3, HC, 0 7145 3993 7, PB, F, 128pp

Rolland, Romain, John Christoper Volume 1, Dawn and Morning, Trans. Gilbert Cannan, J, 1966, -----, PB, F, 209pp

Rolland, Romain, John Christoper Volume 2, Storm and Stress, Trans. Gilbert Cannan, J, 1966, -----, PB, F, 376pp

Rolland, Romain, John Christoper Volume 3, In Paris, Trans. Gilbert Cannan, J, 1966, ----PB, F, 423pp

Rolland, Romain, John Christoper Volume 4, Journey's End, Trans. Gilbert Cannan, J, 1966, -----PB, F, 488pp

Roussel, Raymond, Locus Solus, Trans. Rupert Copeland Cunningham, C&B, 1970, JC, 1983, 0 7145 0661 3, HC, 0 7145 0734 2, PB, F, 254pp

Roussel, Raymond, Impressions of Africa, Trans. Lindy Foord and Rayner Heppenstall, C&B, 1966, JC, 1983, -----HC, 0 7145 0289 8, PB, F, 317pp

Rozewicz, Tadeusz, 'the witnesses & other plays', Trans. Adam Czerniawski, C&B, 1970, 0 7145 0628 1, HC, 0 7145 0629 X, PB, D, 136pp

S

Sachs, Maurice, The Hunt, C&B, (In association with Sidgwick & Jackson), Trans. Richard Howard, 1967, -----HC, F, 176pp

Santos, Luis Martin, Time of Silence, Trans. George Leeson, JC, 1965, -----HC, ----PB, F, 247pp

Sarraute, Nathalie, Portrait of a Man Unknown, Trans. Maria Jolas, Preface by Jean-Paul Sartre, JC, 1959, ------, HC,-------, PB, F,223pp

Sarraute, Nathalie, Martereau, Trans. Maria Jolas, JC, 1964, -------HC, -------PB, F, 250pp

Sarraute, Nathalie, Tropisms and the Age of Suspicion, Trans.Maria Jolas, JC, 1963, ------,HC, ------,PB, F, 136pp

Sarraute, Nathalie, The Planetarium, Trans. Maria Jolas, JC, 1961, J, 1965, ----HC, ------PB, F, 296pp

Schneider, Marcel, Schubert, Trans. Elizabeth Postin, JC, 1959, --------, PB, MB, 190pp

Scott, Walter, Sir, The Supernatural Stories of Sir Walter Scott, editor

Michael Hayes JC 1977 0 7145 3616 4 HC 0 7145 4086 2 PB F 218 pp.

Searle, Chris, Mainland C & B 1974 0 7145 1069 6 HC P 110 pp.

Selbourne, David, 'samson' & 'alison mary fagan', C & B 1971 0 7145 0768 7 HC 0 7145 0769 5 PB D 78 pp.

Shaffer, Anthony, 'sleuth' C & B 1971 0 7145 0762 8 HC 0 7145 0763 6 PB D 94 pp.

Selby, Hubert jr., Last Exit to Brooklyn C & B 1966, reprinted 1966, second edition 1968 ------------- HC C & B :Corgi edition 1970 0 552 08372 0 PB F 234 pp.

Selby, Hubert, jr., The Room C & B 1972 ------- HC F 288 pp.

Semyonov, Julian, TASS is Authorized to Announce JC 1978 0 7145 4120 6 HC F 252 pp.

Semyonov, Julian, Seventeen Moments of Spring JC 1988 0 7145 4140 0 HC F 312 pp.

Shuttle, Penelope, All the Usual Hours of Sleeping C & B 1969 -------HC F 230 pp.

Shuttle, Penelope, Wailing Monkey Embracing a Tree C & B 1973 0 7145 0939 6 HC F 128 pp.

Signature Anthology,   Samuel Beckkett Elspeth Davie Eva Figes Kenneth Gangemi Aidan Higgins Eugene Ionesco Robert Nye Jan Quackenbush Ann Quin Nicholas Rawson C & B 1975 0 7145 0970 1 HC 0 7145 0491 2 PB L 166 pp.

Simon, Claude, The Georgics, trans. Beryl and John Fletcher JC 1989 0 7145 4089 7 HC 0 7145 3897 3 PB F 2432 pp.

Simon, Claude, Triptych trans. Helen R. Lane JC 1977 reprinted 1982, 1986 0 7145 3609 1 HC 0 7145 3787 X PB F 171 pp.

Simon, Claude, The Flanders Road Trans. Richard Howard JC 1985 0 7145 3994 5 PB F 232 pp.

Simon, Claude, The Palace Trans. Richard Howard JC 1987 0 7145 4105 2 PB F 252 pp.Simon, Claude, Conducting Bodies Trans. Helen LM. Lane C & B 1975 0 7145 0331 2 HC 0 7145 0332 0 PB F 192 pp.

Singh, Khushwant, I Shall Not Hear the Nightingale, JC 1959 -----HC -------PB F 242 pp.

Smith, Sydney Goodsir, Collected Poems 1941-1975 JC 1975 0 7145 1105 6 HC 0 7145 3511 7 PB P 269

Smith, Sydney Goodsir, The Wallace, JC 1985 0 7145 4075 7 PB P 180 pp.

Sollers, Philippe, The Park, Trans. A.M.Sheridan Smith, C & B 1968 F 96 pp.

Southern, Terry, Blue Movie C & B 1970 0 7145 0966 3 HC F 288 pp.

Spurling, John, 'in the heart of the british museum', C&B, 1972, 0 7145 0926 4, HC, 0 7145 0927 2, PB, D, 108pp

Spurling, John, 'macrune's guevara', C&B, 1969, ------, HC, ------, PB, D, 116pp.

Stendhal, Rome, Naples and Florence, Trans. Richard N. Coe, JC, 1959, ----HC, -----PB, NF, 256pp

Stendhal, Travels in the South of France, Trans. Elisabeth Abbott, C&B, 1971, 0 7145 0818 7, HC, 0 7145 1108 0, PB,, NF, 276pp

Stendhal, Selected Journalism- From the English Reviews, Editor Geoffrey Strickland, JC, 1959, ---------PB, NF, 341pp

Stendhal, Lives of Haydn, Mozart and Metastasio, Trans. Richard N. Coe, C&B, 1972, 0 7145 0349 5, HC, 0 7145 0350 9, PB, NF, 370pp.

Sternheim, Carl, Plays,The Bloomers, The Snob, Paul Schippel, 1913, The

Fossil, Trans. M.A.L.Brown, M.A. McHaffie, J.M. Ritchie, J.D. Stowell, C&B, 1970, 0 7145 0026 7, HC, 0 7145 0027 5, PB, D, 285pp

Stevenson, Robert Louis, The Supernatural Short Stories, Edited Michael Hayes, JC, 1976, 0 7145 3550 8, HC, F, 182pp

Stonehouse, John, The Baring Fault, JC, 1986, 0 7145 4069 2, HC, 0 7145 4106 0, PB, F, 432pp

Storey, Anthony, Jesus Iscariot, C&B, 1967, ------HC, -----, PB, F, 204pp.

Storey, Anthony, The Centre Holds, C&B, 1973, 0 7145 0902 7, F, 168pp

Storey, Anthony, Platium Jag, C&B, 1972, 0 7145 0901 9, HC, 0 7145 0951 5, PB, F, 142pp

Storey, Anthony, Graceless Goi, C&B, 1969, ----HC, 0 7145 0052 6, F, 172pp.

Storey, Anthony, The Rector, C&B, 1970, 0 7145 0726 1, HC 0 7145 0727 X, PB, F, 176pp

Storm, Theodor, Viola Tricolor and Curator Carsten, Trans. Byard Quincy Morgan and Frieda M. Voigt, JC, 1956, HC, -------, --------,PB, F, 118pp

Super, R.H., Walter Savage Landor: A Biography, JC, 1957, ------, HC, B, 654pp

Sutherland, Millie, The Brae House, JC, 1979, 0 7145 3646 6, HC, B, 195pp

T

Three German Classics, Immensee, Theodor, Storm, Trans. Ronald Taylor/ Lenz, Georg Buckner, Trans. Michael Hamburger/ A Village Romeo and Juiliet, Gottfried Keller, Trans. Ronald Taylor, C&B, 1966, JC, 1985, ------HC, 0 7145 0561 7, PB, 188pp

Tiger, Virginia, William Golding: The Dark Fields of Discovery, C&B, 1974, 0 7145 1012 2, HC, LC, 244pp

Tolstoy, Leo, The Devil& Family Happiness, Trans. April FitzLyon, S&C, 1953, Second Impression, 1954, -----HC, ------PB, F, 214pp

Topor, Roland, Leonardo Was Right, Trans. Barbara Wright, JC, 1978, 0 7145 3671 7, PB, D, 25pp.

Topor, Roland, Joko's Anniversary, Trans. J.A. Underwood, C&B, 1970, 0 7145 0684 2, HC, 0 7145 0685 0, PB, F, 124pp

Trocchi, Alexander, Man at Leisure, C&B, 1972, 0 7145 0357 6, HC, 0 7145 0358 4, PB, P, 90pp

Trocchi, Alexander, Cain's Book, JC, 1963, J, 1963, CP, 1992, ---------, HC, 0 7145 4233 4, PB,F, 252pp

Trocchi, Alexander, Young Adam, JC, 1983, 0 7145 3925 2, PB, F, 160pp

Tucker, Eva, Contact, C&B, 1966, -----HC, ------, PB, F, 158pp

Tucker, Eva, Drowning, C&B, 1969, ------HC, F, 188pp

Tusquets, Esther, Love is a Solitary Game, Trans. Bruce Pennman, JC, 1985, 0 7145 4042 0, PB, F, 144pp.

Tzara, Tristan, Seven Dada Manifestos, Trans. Barbara Wright, JC, 1977, 1981, 0 7145 3557 5, HC, 0 7145 3762 4, PB, NF, 115pp.

V

Valentine, Alan, The Education of an American, JC, 1957, ------HC, ------, PB, NF, 284pp

Vestdijk, Simon, Rum Island, Trans. BK. Bowes, JC, 1963, ----HC, -----PB, F, 376pp.

Volponi, Paolo, The Worldwide Machine, Trans. Belen Sevarid, C&B, 1969, ---- HC, F, 215pp

Volponi, Paolo, The Memorandum, Trans. Belen Sevarid, C&B, 1967, ------ HC, 0 7145 0377 0, PB, F, 231pp

W

Walser, Martin, Plays, The Rabbit Race & The Detour, Trans. Richard Gruenberger, JC, 1963, -----HC, ------PB, D, 172pp

Walser, Martin, The Unicorn, Trans. Barrie Ellis-Jones, C&B, 1971, 0 7145 0817 9, HC, 0 7145 0886 1, PB, F, 284pp

Walser, Robert, The Walk and other stories, Trans. Christopher Middleton, JC, 1957, -----HC, ------, PB, F, 104pp

Wedekind, Frank, The Lulu Plays & other Sex Tragedies, Earth Spirit, Pandora's Box, Death and Devil Wetterstein, Trans. Stephen Spender, C&B, 1972, 0 7145 0867 5, HC, 0 7145 0868 3, PB, D, 282pp

Wedekind, Frank, 'spring awakening' Trans. Tom Osborn, C&B, 1969, Reprinted 1977, 1978, 1981, 1985, 0 7145 0633 8, HC, 0 7145 0634 6, PB, D, 84pp

Weiss, Peter, The Persecution and Assasination of Marat as Performed by the Inmates of the Asylm of Charenton Under the Direction of Marquis of Sade, English Version, Geoffrey Skelton, Verse Adaptation by Adrien Mitchell, JC, 1965, ----HC, ------PB, D, 124pp

Weiss, Peter, The Investigation: Oratorio in 11 Cantos, English Version Alexander Gross, C&B, 1966, ------HC, D, 206pp

Weiss, Peter, 'discourse on vietnam', Trans. Geoffrey Skelton, C&B, 1971, 0 7145 0747 4, HC, 0 7145 0748 2, PB, D, 190pp

Weiss, Peter, Leave Taking & Vanishing Point, Trans. Christopher Levenson, C&B, 1966, ----HC, 0 7145 0337 1, PB, F, 275pp

Weiss, Peter, The Conversation of the Three Walkers and The Shadow of the Coachman's Body, Trans. S.M. Cupitt, C&B, 1972, 0 7145 0180 8, HC, F, 168pp

Weiss, Peter, Notes on the Cultural Life of the Democratic Republic of Vietnam, C&B, 1971, 0 7145 0739 3, HC, 0 714 0740 7, PB, NF, 180pp

Welburn, Vivienne C., 'johnny so long & the drag' C&B, 1967, ------HC, ------ PB, D, 135pp

Welburn, Vivienne C., 'the treadwheel' & 'coil without dreams', C&B, 1975, 0 7145 099 X, HC, 0 7145 1009 9, PB, D, 192pp

Welburn, Vivienne C., 'clearway', C&B, 1967, -------HC, -----PB, D, 100pp

Wilkinson, Elizabeth N., Editor, Goethe Revisited: A Collection of Essays, JC, 1984, 0 7145 3951 1, PB, NF, 192pp

Williams, Denis, The Third Temptation, C&B, 1968, -------HC, F, 118pp

Williams, Heathcote, The Immoralist, JC, 1978, 0 7145 3714 4, PB, D, 39pp

Williams, Heathcote, AC/DC, C&B, 1972, 0 7145 0889 6, HC, 0 7145 0890 X, PB, D, 137pp

Wilson, Colin, 'strindberg', C&B, 1970, 0 7145 0639 7, HC, 0 7145 0640 0, PB, D, 78pp

Wilson, Snoo, 'the number of the beast' & 'flaming bodies', JC, 1983, 0 7145 3959 7, PB, D, 92pp

Wilson, Snoo, 'pig night' & 'blow job', JC, 1975, 0 7145 3503 6, HC, 0 7145 3509 5, PB, D, 86pp

Wingfield, Sheila, Her Storms: Selected Poems 1938-1977, The Dolmen Press/JC, 0 7145 3674 1, HC, P, 128pp

Wingfield, Shelia, Admissions: Poems, 1974-1977, The Doleman Press/JC, 1977, 0 7145 3673 3, HC, P, 61pp

Wolkers, Jan, Turkish Delight, Trans. Greta Kilburn, C&B, 1974, 0 7145 1055 6, HC, F, 158pp

Wright, Sarah E., This Child's Gonna Live, C&B, 1969, 0 7145 0556 0, HC, F, 276pp

Wykham, Helen, Ribstone Pippins, Allen Figgis/C&B, 1974, ------HC, F, 226pp

Wymark, Olwen, 'the gymnasium' & other plays, C&B, 1971, 0 7145 0794 6, HC, 0 7145 0795 4, PB, D, 144pp

Wymark, Olwen, Three Plays, Lunchtime Concert, The Inhabitants, Coda, C&B, 71967, -------HC, -------,PB, D, 82pp

Wymark, Olwen, 'best friends,' 'the committee', 'the twenty second day', JC, 1984, 0 7145 3955 4, D, 72pp

Wynne, John, Crime Wave, JC, 1982, 0 86676000 8, HC, F, 203pp

Wynne-Tyson, Jon, Marvellous Party, JC, 1989, 0 7145 4178 8, PB, D, 93pp

Y

Yavin, Naftali, 'precious moments from the family album to provide you with comfort in the long years to come', C&B, 1969, 0 7145 0635 4, HC, 0 7145 0636 2, PB, D, 106pp

Yevtushenko, Yevgeny, The Poetry of Yevgeny Yevtushenko 1953 to 1965, Trans. George Reavey, Bilingual Edition, C&B, 1966, ------HC, -------PB, P, 213pp

Yevtushenko, Yevgeny, The Poetry of Yevgeny Yevtushenko: Revised and Enlarged Edition, Edited, Trans. With Introduction, George Reavey, C&B, 1969, 07145 0481 5, HC, 0 7145 0482 3, PB, P, 274pp

Z

Zola, Emile, Ladies Delight, Trans. April FitzLyon, JC, 1957, ------HC, F, 407pp

Beckett Bibliography

In Chronological Order

Dream of Fair to middling Women, Edited by Eoin O'Brien and Edith Fournier, CP, 1993, 0 7145 4212 1, HC, 0 7145 4213 X, PB, F, 241pp

Proust and Three Dialogues, With Georges Duthuit, JC, 1965, C&B, 1970, JC, 1976, -------HC, 0 7145 0034 8, PB, F, 126pp

More Pricks Than Kicks, C&B, 1970, 1973, CP, 1993, 0 7145 0704 0, HC, 0 7145 0705 9, PB, F, 204pp

Murphy, J, 1963, JC, 1977, 0 7145 0041 0, HC, 0 7145 0042 9, PB, F, 158pp

Watt, J, 1963, C&B, 1970, JC, 1976, Reprinted 1978, 1981, 1998, 0 7145 0609 5, HC, 0 7145 0610 9, PB, F, 255pp

Mercier and Camier, Trans. by the author, C&B, 1974, 0 7145 1091 2, HC, 0 7145 1139 0, PB, F, 123pp

First Love, Trans. by the Author, C&b, 1973, 0 7145 0965 5, HC, 0 7145 1124 2, PB, F, 62pp

Four Novellas, First Love, The Expelled, The Calmative, The End, JC, 1977, 0 7145 3612 1, HC, F, 94pp

Malone Dies, Trans. by the Author, JC, 1958, Reissued in PB, C&B, 1968, -------- HC, 0 7145 0858 6, PB, F, 120pp

Malone Dies, Trans. by the Author, C&B, 1975, JC, 1987, 0 7145 0858 6, PB, F, 117pp

Molloy Malone Dies The Unnamable, JC, 1959, C&B, 1966, CP, 1994, 0 7145 1053 X, HC, F, 418pp

Molloy Malone Dies The Unnamable, C&B, 1966, 1973, JC, 1976, CP, 1994, 0 7145 1053 X, PB, F, 418pp

Anthology of Mexican Poetry, Trans. by Samuel Beckett, Compiled by Octavio Paz, Preface by C.M. Bowra, C&B, 1970, 0 7145 0086 0, HC, 0 7145 0086 0, PB, P, 213pp

Poems in English, JC, 1961, C&B, 1968, Reprinted 1971, 0 7145 0477 7, HC, 0 7145 0478 5, PB, P, 53pp

Zone, by Guillaume Apollinaire with an English Translation by Samuel Beckett, The Dolman Press Dublin, London: C&B, 1972, 0 7145 0866 7, HC, P, 23pp

Texts For Nothing, Trans. by the Author, C&B, 1974, 0 7145 0984 1, HC, 0 7145 0985 X, PB, F, 64pp

How It Is, Trans by the Author, JC, 1964, C&B, 1972, JC, 1977, 1996, -------HC, 0 7145 0952 3, PB, F, 160pp

All Strange Away, JC, 1979, 0 7145 3748 9, HC, 0 7145 3858 2, PB, F, 44pp

Imagination Dead Imagine, Trans. by the Author, C&B, 1965, --------PB, F, 14pp

Six Residua, JC, 1978, 0 7145 3633 4, HC, 0 7145 3663 6, PB, F, 79pp

The Lost Ones, Trans. by the Author, C&B, 1972, 0 7145 0891 8, HC, 0 7145 0892 6, PB, F, 63pp

For To End Yet Again and other fizzles, JC, 1976, 0 7145 3599 0, HC, 0 7145 3600 8, PB, F, 54pp

Come and Go Dramaticule, C&B, 1967, --------PB, D, 10pp

Lessness, C&B, 1970, 0 7145 0682 6, HC, 0 7145 0683 4, PB, F, 21pp

Collected Poems in English and French, JC, 1977, 0 7145 3608 3, HC, 0 7145

3613 X, PB, P, 147pp
Company, JC, 1980, 0 7145 3806 X, HC, 0 7145 3857 4, PB, F, 89pp
Ill Seen Ill Said, Trans. by the Author, JC, 1982, Reprinted 1997, 0 7145 3895 7, HC, 0 7145 3895 2, PB, F, 159pp
Worstward Ho, JC, 1983, 0 7145 3979 1, HC, 0 7145 4006 4, PB, F, 47pp
Disjecta: Miscellaneous Writings and A Dramatic Fragment, Edited with a foreword by Ruby Cohn, JC, 1983, 0 7145 3974 0, HC, 0 7145 4016 1, PB, F, 178pp
Nohow On Company Ill Seen Ill Said Worstward Ho, JC, 1989, 0 7145 4111 7, HC, 0 7145 4112 5, PB, F, 128pp
Collected Poems 1930-1978, JC, 1984, 0 7145 4052 8, HC, 0 7145 4053 8, PB, P, 179pp
Collected Shorter Prose 1945-1980, JC, 1984, 0 7145 4027 7, HC, 0 7145 4033 1, PB, F, 218pp
As the Story Was Told Uncollected and Late Prose, JC, 1990, 0 7145 4113 3, HC, F, 134pp
Stirrings Still, Illustrated by Louis leBrocquy, Blue Moon Books, New York, John Calder London, 1988, 0 7145 4142 7, Unpaginated

Books About Beckett

Calder, John Editor, A Samuel Beckett Reader, C&B, 1967, --------HC, F, 192pp
McMillian, Dougald and Fehsenfeld, Martha, Beckett in the Theatre, JC, 1988, 0 7145 3952 X, HC, 0 7145 4151 6, PB, LC, 333pp
Beckett at 60: A Festschrift, C&B, 1967, --------HC, LC, 99pp
As No Other Dare Fail: For Samuel Beckett on his Eightieth Birthday by His Friends and Admirers, JC, 1986, 0 7145 4077 3, HC, LC, 136pp
Kenner, Hugh, Samuel Beckett: A Critical Study, JC, 1962, ------HC, ---PB, LC, 212pp
Knowlson, James and Pilling, John, Frescoes of the Skull: The Later Prose and Drama of Samuel Beckett, JC, 1979, 0 7145 3643 1, HC, LC, 292pp

From 1976 to The Journal of Beckett Studies was published by John Calder (Publishers) Ltd and the Beckett Archive at the University of Reading

Journal of Beckett Studies ISSN 0309 5207

Number 1 Winter 1976, 114pp
Number 2 Summer 1977, 138pp
Number 3 Summer 1978, 137pp
Number 4 Spring 1979, 114pp
Number 5, Autumn, 1979, 158pp
Number 6 Autumn, 1980, 160pp
Number 7 Spring 1982, 158pp
Number 8 Autumn 1982, 160pp
Number 9 (1984), 154pp
Number 10 (1985), 176pp

Number 11 and 12 -- Special Double Issue, 1989, 224pp

Music Books

Opera Annual, 1954-1955, Edited by Harold Rosenthal, Introduction by The Earl of Harewood, JCP, 1954, -------HC, O, 184pp
Opera Annual 1955-1956, Edited by Harold Rosenthal, Intro. Irmgard Seefried, JC, 1955, -------HC, O, 176pp
Opera Annual No. 3, Edited by Harold Rosenthal, JC, 1956, ----HC, O, 190pp
Opera Annual No. 4, Edited by Harold Rosenthal, JC, 1957, ------HC, O, 188pp
Opera Annual No. 5, Edited by Harold Rosenthal, JC, 1958, ------HC, O, 208pp
Opera Annual No. 6, Edited by Harold Rosenthal, JC, 1959, ------HC, O, 204pp
Opera Annual No. 7, Edited by Harold Rosenthal, JC, 1960, -------HC, ------PB, O, 218pp
Opera Annual No. 8, Edited by Harold Rosenthal, JC, 1962, --------HC, O, 144pp
Cage, John, M: Writings - 67-72, C&B, 1973, 0 7145 1135 8, PB, 0 7145 0976 0, HC, M, 217pp
Cage, John, A Year From Monday: New Lectures and Writings, C&B, 1968, -------HC, 0 7145 0621 4, PB, M, 168pp
Cage, John, Silence: Lectures and Writings, C&B, 1968, 0 7145 0526 9,HC, 0 7145 1043 2, PB, M, 276pp
Charters, Samuel, The Legacy of the Blues, C&B, 1975, 0 7145 1098 X, HC, 0 7145 1099 8, PB, M, 192pp
Cooper, Peter, Style in Piano Playing, JC, 1975, 0 7145 3512 5, HC, M, 182pp
Eaton, Quaintence, Opera Caravan: Adventures of the Metropolitian on Tour, 1883-1956, Foreword by Rudolpf Bing, JC, 1957(Sponsored by the Metropolitan Opera Guild) ------HC, O, 400pp
Ellison, Mary, Extensions of the Blues, JC, 1989, 0 7145 3717 9, HC, 0 7145 3846 9, PB, M, 307pp
Ewen, David, Encyclopaedia of the Opera, JC, 1956, Reprinted 1960, Revised Enlarged Edition, C&B, 1971, O, 594pp
Fellner, Rudolph, Opera Themes and Plots, Preface Erich Liensdorf, JC, 1958, ---------HC, O, 354pp
Fuchs, Viktor, The Art of Singing and Voice Technique, Introduction by Lauritz Melchior, JC, 1963, C&B 1967, Second Revised Edition C&B, 1973, JC 1985, 0 7145 0031 3, HC, 0 7145 0032 1, PB, M, 219pp
Garten, H.F., Wagner: The Dramatist, JC, 1977, 0 7145 3620 2, HC, O, 160pp
Gatti-Casazza, Giulio, Memories of the Opera, JC, 1977, 0 7145 3518 4, HC, 0 7145 3665 2, PB, O, 326pp
Harding, James, Jacques Offenbach: A Biography, JC, 1980, 0 7145 3835 3, HC, 0 7145 3841 8, PB, MB, 274pp
Hell, Heni, Frances Poulenc, Trans. Edward Lockspeiser, JC, 1959, -------HC, MB, 118pp
Hofmann, Michel R., Tchaikovsky, Trans. Angus Heriot, JCP, 1962, --------HC, ------PB, MB, 192pp
Hoffnung, Gerard, The Hoffnung Music Festival, R, 1984, 0 86676 007 5, PB,

M, Unpaginated

Hoffnung, Gerard, The Hoffnung Symphony Orchestra, R, 1984, 0 86676 008 3, PB, M, Unpaginated

Heriot, Angus, The Castrati in Opera, JCP, 1960, C&B, 1975, 0 7145 0153 0, HC, 0 7145 0154 9, PB, M, 243pp

Hollander, Hans, Leos Janacek: His Life and Work, Trans. Paul Hamburger, JC, 1963, -----HC, ------PB, MB, 222pp

Ives, Charles E., Memos, Edited by John Kirkpatrick, C&B, 1973, 0 7145 0953 1, HC, 0 7145 0954 X, PB, M, 355pp

Ives, Charles, Essays Before a Sonata and Other Writings, Edited by Howard Boatwright, C&B, 1969, ------HC, 0 7145 0219 7, PB, M, 258pp

Krenek, Ernst, Exploring Music: Essays, Trans. Margaret Shenfield & Jeoffrey Skelton, C&B, 1966, -------HC, 0 7145 0226 X, M, 245pp

Leider, Frida, Playing My Part, C&B, 1966, -------HC, M, 217pp

Liebner, Janos, Mozart on the Stage, C&B, 1972, 0 7145 0758 X, HC, 0 7145 1070 X, PB, M, 254pp

Liess, Andres, Carl Orff: His Life and His Music, Trans. Adeleheid and Herbert Parkin, C&B, 1966, ------HC, 0 7145 0152 2, PB, MB, 184pp

Lockspeiser, Edward, Compiled and Edited, The Literary Clef: An Anthology of Letters and Writings by French Composers, jC, 1958, -----HC, ------PB, M, 186pp

Loewenberg, Alfred, Compiled, Annals of Opera, 1597-1940, Introduction by Edward J. Dent, JC, 1978, Third Edition Revised and Corrected, 0 7145 3657 1, HC, M, 1755pp

Milhaud, Darius, Notes Without Music: An Autobiography, Trans. Donald Evans, Edited by Rollo H. Myers, C&B, 1970, -------, PB, M, 258pp

Mueller, John H., The American Symphony Orchestra: A Social History of Musical Taste, JC, 1958, ------HC, M, 437pp

Myers, Rollo H., Editor, Twentieth Century Music, JC, 1960, C&B, 1968, Second Revised and Enlarged Edition, ------HC, 0 7145 0588 9, PB, M, 287pp

Newman, Ernest, From The World of Music: Essays from the Sunday Times, Selected by Felix Aprahamian, JC, 1956, ------HC, M, 190pp

Newman, Ernest, Volume One: Essays from the World of Music, Selected by Felix Aprahamian, JC, 1976, (Orginally published in 1956) 0 7145 3548 6, HC, 0 7145 3587 7, PB, M, 190pp

Newman, Ernest, Volume Two: More Essays from the World of Music, Selected by Felix Aprahamian, JC, 1976, (Originally published in 1958) 0 7145 3549 4, HC, 0 7145 3598 2, PB, M, 259pp

Ouelette, Fernand, Edgard Varese, Trans. Derek Coltman, C&B, 1973, 0 7145 0208 1, HC, 0 7145 0209 X, PB, B, 270pp

Petit, Pierre, Verdi, Trans. Patrick Bowles, JCP, 1962, -------HC, --------PB, B, 192pp

Prey, Herman, First Night Fever: The Memoirs of Herman Prey, Written with the Help of Robert D. Abraham, Trans. Andrew Shackleton, JC, 1986, 0 7145 3998 8, HC, 0 7145 4102 8, PB, M, 288pp

Redlich, H.F., Alban Berg: The Man and His Music, JC, 1957, -------HC, B, 316pp

Redwood, Christopher, Editor, A Delius Companion, JC, 1976, 0 7145 3526 5, HC, 0 7145 3826 4, PB, M, 270pp

Rognoni, Luigi, The Second Vienna School: The Rise of Expressionism in the Music of Arnold Schoenberg, Alban Berg and Anton von Webern, Trans. Robert W. Mann, JC, 1977, 0 7145 3528 1, HC, 0 7145 3865 5, PB, M, 417pp

Rosenthal, Harold, Great Singers of Today, C&B, 1966, -------HC, M, 212pp

Rosenthal, Harold, Sopranos of Today: Studies of Twenty-Five Opera Singers, JC, 1956, ----HC, O, 103pp

Ross, Anne, Editor, The Opera Directory, JC, 1961, -----HC, O, 566pp

Rostand, Claude, Liszt, Trans. John Victor, C&B, 1972, 0 7145 0342 8, HC, 0 7145 0343 6, PB, B, 192pp

Sadie, Stanley, Handel, JCP, 1962, -------HC, ------, PB, B, 192pp

Sadie, Stanley, Mozart, C&B, 1965, -------HC, ------, PB, B, 192pp

Samuel, Claude, Prokofiev, C&B, 1971, 0 7145 0489 0, HC, 0 7145 0490 4, PB, B, 192pp

Siohan, Robert, Stravinski, Trans. Éric Walter White, C&B, 1965, 0 7145 0070 4, PB, ------, HC, B, 192pp

Schonzeler, Hans-Hubert, Bruckner, C&B, 1970, 0 7145 0144 1, HC, 0 7145 0145 X, PB, B, 190pp

Seroff, Victor I., Debussy: Musician of France, JC, 1957, ------HC, B, 367pp

Small, Christoper, Music Society Education, JC, 1977, Second Revised Edition, 1980, Second Impression, 1984, 0 7145 3530 3, HC, 0 7145 3614 8, PB, M, 234pp

Small, Christopher, Music of the Common Tongue: Survival and Celebration in Afro-American Music, JC, 1987, JCP, 1994, 0 7145 4095 1, HC, 0 7145 4096 X, PB, M, 495pp

Stendhal, Lives of Hayden, Mozart and Metastasio, Trans., Intoduced and Edited by Richard N. Coe, C&B, 1972, 0 7145 0349 5, HC, 0 7145 0350 9, PB, M, 370pp

Stendhal, Life of Rossini, Trans. Richard N. Coe, JC, 1956, New and Revised Edition; Trans and Annotated by Richard N. Coe, C&B, 1970, JC, 1985, 0 7145 0341 X, HC, 0 7145 0632 X, PB, B, 566pp

Stravinski, Igor, An Autobiography, C&B, 1975, 0 7145 1063 7, HC, 0 7145 1082 3, PB, M, 180pp

Stuckenschmidt, H.H., Ferruccio Busoni: Chronicle of a European, Trans. Sandra Morris, C&B, 1970, 0 7145 0234 0, HC, 0 7145 0235 9, PB, B, 224pp

Stuckenschmidt, H.H., Arnold Schoenberg, Trans. Edith Temple Roberts and Humphrey Searle, JC, 1959, -----HC, ------, PB, B, 168pp

Stuckenschmidt, H.H., Arnold Schoenberg: His Life, World and Work, Trans. Humphrey Searle, JC, 1977, 0 7145 3532 X, HC, 0 7145 3864 7, PB, B, 582pp

Stuckenschmidt, H.H., Maurice Ravel: Variations on His Life and Work, Trans. Samuel R. Rosenbaum, C&B, 1969, 0 7145 0024 0, HC, 0 7145 0025 9, PB, B, 272pp

Strauss, Richard, and Rolland, Romain, Correspondence, Edited by Rollo Myers, C&B 1968, -------HC, 0 7145 0503 X, PB, M, 240pp

Turing, Penelope, Hans Hotter: Man and Artist, JC, 1983, 0 7145 3988 0, HC, 0 7145 4091 6, PB, B, 280pp

Wade, Graham, Traditions of the Classical Guitar, JC, 1980, 0 7145 3794 2, HC, 0 7145 3913 9, PB, M, 270pp

Wallace, Ian, Promise Me You'll Sing Mud! The Autobiography, JC, 1975, 0 7145 3500 1, HC, 0 7145 3594 X, PB, M, 236pp

Walsh, T.J., Second Empire Opera: The Theatre Lyrique , Paris 1851-1870,

JC, 1981, 0 7145 3659 8, HC, M, 384pp

Wechsberg, Joseph, The Violin, C&B, 1973, 0 7145 1020 3, HC, M, 314pp

Wildgans, Friedrich, Anton Webern, Trans. Edith Temple Roberts and Humphrey Searle, C&B, 1966, B, 185pp

Williamson, Audrey, Wagner Opera, JCP, 1962, JC, 1981 Second Revised Edition, -----HC, 0 7145 0603 6, PB, B, 192pp

Poltical Books

Abrahams, Gerald, Morality & The Law, C&B, 1971, 0 7145 0662 1, HC, 0 7145 0663 X, PB, NF, 231pp.

Adler, Mortimer J., What Man Has Made of Man, JC, 1957, -----HC, NF, 246pp

Alleg, Henri, The Question, Trans., John Calder, Preface, Jean Paul Sartre, JC, 1958, --------HC, NF, 96pp

Altrinchan, Lord, and others, Is the Monarchy Perfect? JC, 1958, -----HC, NF, 151pp

Baker, Capt. Peter, My Testament, JC, 1957, -------HC, NF, 288pp

Baran, Paul A., The Political Economy of Growth, JC, 1957, -----HC, NF, 308pp

Baumann, Bommi, Terror or Love? The Personal Account of a West German Urban Guerrilla, Trans. Helene Ellenbogen & Wayne Parker, JC, 1979, 0 7145 3779 9, HC, 0 7145 3782 9, PB, NF, 128pp

Bernard, Jessie, The Future of Parenthood, C&B, 1975, 0 7145 0428 9, HC, NF, 426pp

Boyer, Richard O. & Morais Herbert M., A History of the American Labour Movement, JC, 1956, -------HC, NF, 402pp

Boyle, Godfrey, Living on the Sun: Harnessing Renewable Energy for an Equitable Society, C&B, 1975, 0 7145 1094 7, HC, 0 7145 0862 4, PB, NF, 128pp

Brée, Germaine, Camus and Sartre: Crisis and Commitment, C&B, 1974, 0 7145 1011 4, PB, NF, 288pp

Buchan, Alasdair, The Right To Work: The Story of the Upper Clyde Confrontation, C&B, 1972, 0 7145 0934 5, HC, 0 7145 0935 3, PB, NF, 160pp

Burns, James MacGregor, The Deadlock of Democracy: Four-Party Politics in America, JC, 1964, -----HC, NF, 376pp.

Calne, Sir Roy, Too Many People, CP, 1994, 0 7145 4269 5, PB, NF, 144pp.

Caprio, Frank S., Variations in Sexual Behaviour, JC, 1957, Fourth Impression 1961,Sixth Impression 1966, -------HC, 0 7145 0772 5, PB, NF, 344pp

Chapin, John, Editor, The Book of Catholic Quotations, JC, 1957, ---------HC, NF, 1074pp

Cordero, Franco, Against the Catholic System, Trans. Anthony Johnson; C&B, 1972, 0 7145 0936 1, HC, NF, 144pp

Cushing, Red, Soldier for Hire, JC, 1962, -------HC, NF, 296pp

Fisher, Seymour, Body Consciousness, C&B 1973, 0 7145 1000 9, HC, 0 7145 1001 7, PB, NF, 176pp

Florey, R.A., The General Strike of 1926: The Economic, Political and

Social Causes of That Class War, JC, 1980 , 07145 3698 9, HC, 0 7145 3698 9, PB, nF, 222pp

Gangrene, Introduction by Peter Beneson, JC, 1959, -------PB, NF, 157pp

Cyr, Arthur, Liberal Party Politics in Britian, JC, 1977, 0 7145 3546 X, HC, 0 7145 3611 3, PB, NF, 320pp

Dalton, David, Janis, C&B and Nel, 1972, 0 7145 0943 4, HC, NF, 154pp

Hain, Peter, Editor, Community Polics, 1976, 0 7145 3537 0, HC, 0 7145 3543 5, PB, NF, 225pp

Hain, Peter, Editor, Humphrey, Derek, Rose-Smith, Brian, Policing the Police, JC, 1979, 0 7145 3624 5, HC, 0 7145 3628 8, PB, NF, 196pp

Heilbroner, Robert L., An Inquiry into the Human Prospect, C&B, 1975, 0 7145 0932 9, HC, 0 7145 0933 7, PB, NF, 150pp

Heschel, Abraham, J., God in Search of Man: A Philsophy of Judiasm, JC, 1956, -----HC, NF, 438pp

International Literary Annual No. 2, John Wain Editor, JC, 1959, -------, HC, ------PB, NF, 246pp

International Literary Annual no. 3, Arthur Boyars and Pamela Lyon, Editors, JC, 1961, -------hC, ------, PB, NF, 230pp

International Film Annual No. 1, Campbell Dixon, Editor, JC, 1957, ------HC, NF, 167pp

Internatioonal Film Annual No. 2, William Whitebait, Editor, JC; 1959, ------HC, NF, 181pp

International Theatre Annual No. 1, Harold Hobson Editor, JC, 1956, -------HC, NF, 174pp

International Theatre Annual No. 2, Harold Hobson, Editor, JC, 1957, ------HC, NF, 220pp

International Theatre Annual No. 3, Harold Hobson, Editor, JC, 1958, ------HC, NF, 232pp

International Theatre Annual No. 4, Harold Hobson, Editor, JC, 1959, ------HC, NF, 288pp

International Theatre Annual, No. 5, Harold Hobson Editor, JC, 1961, ------HC, ------PB, NF, 274pp

Hiss, Alger, In the Court of Public Opinion, JC, 1957, -----PB, NF, 424pp

Hoch, Paul, The Newspaper Game: The Political Sociology of the Press, C&B, 1974, 0 7145 0857 8, HC, 0 7145 1125 0, PB, 217pp

Hofman, Werner, Caricature: From Leonardo to Picasso, JC 1957 -------HC NF 150 pp.

Hutchison, Commander E.H., Violent Truce: The Arab-Israeli Conflict 1951-1955, JC 1956 -------HC NF 199pp.

Illich, Ivan, Tools for Conviviality, C & B 1973 0 7145 0973 6 HC 0 7145 0974 4 PB NF 112 pp.

Illich, Ivan, Medical Nemesis: The Exploration of Health, C B 1975 0 7145 1095 5 HC 0 7145 1096 3 PB NF 184 pp.

Illich, Ivan D., Celebration of Awareness: A Call for Institional Revolution, Introduction by Erich Fromm, C&B, 1971, 0 7145 0837 3, HC, 0 7145 0838 1, PB, NF, 192pp

Illich, Ivan D., Deschooling Society, C&B, 1971, 0 7145 0878 0, HC, 0 7145 0879 9, PB, NF, 118pp

Illich, Ivan D., Energy and Equity, C&B, 1974, 0 7145 1057 2, HC, 0 7145 1058

0, PB, NF, 96pp

Jefferson, Michael, White, Andrew Dickson, Mann, Thomas, Rostow, Walt, Inflation, JC, 1977, 0 7145 3539 7, HC, 0 7145 3547 8, PB, NF, 192pp

Julien, Claude, Suicide of the Democracy, Trans. J.A. Underwood, C&B, 1975, 0 7145 1061 0, HC, NF, 272pp

Jungk, Robert, The Nuclear State, Trans. Éric Mosbacher, JC 1979, 0 7145 3680 6, HC, 0 7145 3689 X, PB, NF, 178PP

Kingston, William, Innovation: The Creative Impulse in Human Progress, JC, 1977, 0 7145 3540 0, HC, 0 7145 3611 3, PB, NF, 160pp

Lamont, Corliss, Freedom is as Freedom Does, Foreword Bertrand Russell, JC, 1956, ----HC, NF, 322pp

Lilly, John C., The Centre of the Cyclone: An Autobiography of Inner Space, C&B, 1973, 0 7145 0961 2, HC, NF, 220pp

Linhart, Robert, The Assembly Line, Trans. Margaret Crosland, JC, 1981, 0 7145 3742 X, PB, NF, 160pp

Lucie-Smith, Edward, Thinking About Art: Critical Essays, C&B, 1968, -------- HC, NF, 238pp

Mercer, John, Scotland: The Devolution of Power, JC, 1978, 0 7145 3622 9, HC, 0 7145 3627 X, PB, NF, 250pp

Milne, Edward, No Shining Armour, JC, 1997, 0 7145 3501 X, HC, 0 7145 3514 1, PB, NF, 264pp

Navasky, Victor S., Naming Names, JC, 1982, 0 7145 3902 2, PB, NF, 482pp

Noel-Baker, Phillip, The Arms Race: A Programme for World Disarment, JCP, 1958, --------PB, NF, 604pp

Quinliven, Patrick and Rose, Paul, The Phineans In England 1865-1872: A Sense of Insecurity, JC, 1982, 0 7145 3575 6, PB, NF, 198pp

Rey, Benoist, The Throat Cutters, Trans. G. Lobbenberg, JC, 1961, -----HC, NF, 128pp

Robertson, James, Prophet or People? The New Social Role of Money, C&B, 1974, 0 7145 0848 9, HC, 0 7145 0773 3, PB, NF, 96pp

Formann, Lionel and Sachs, E.S. (Solly), The South African Treason Trial, JC, 1957,-----HC, NF, 216pp

Sandford, Jeremy, Smiling David: The Story of David Oluwale, C&B, 1974, 0 7145 1048 3, HC, 0 7145 1049 1, PB, NF, 112pp

Searle, Chris, This New Season: Our Class, Our Schools, Our World, C&B, 1973, 0 7145 0972 8, HC, 0 7145 1047 5, PB, NF, 192pp

Searle, Chris, Mainland, C&B, 1974, 0 7145 1069 6, PB, P, 110pp

Smedley, Agnes, The Great Road: The Life and Times of Chu Teh, JC, 1958, -------HC, NF, 462pp

Smith, N.A., The New Enlightenment: An Essay in Political Realism, JC, 1976, 0 7145 3593 1, HC, 0 7145 3604 0, PB, NF, 256pp

Swartz, Harry, The Layman's Medical Dictionary, JC, 1955, -------HC, NF, 306pp

Szasz, Thomas S., Ideology and Insanity: Essays on the Psychiatic Dehumanization of Man, C&B, 1973, 0 7145 0958 2, HC, 0 7145 1054 8, PB, NF, 264pp

Talese, Gay, The Kingdom and the Power, C&B, 1971, 0 7145 0746 6, HC, ------PB, NF, 555pp

Tomlinson, John, Left-Right: The March of Political Extremism in Britian,

JC, 1981, 0 7145 3855 8, PB, NF, 152pp

Tomkinson, Martin, and Gillard, Michael, Nothing to Declare: The Political Corruptions of John Poulson, JC, 1980, 0 7145 3625 3, HC, 0 7145 3629 6, PB, NF, 340pp

Ullerstam, Lars, The Erotic Minorites: A Swedish View, C&B, 1967, -----HC, 0 7145 0791 1, PB, NF, 146pp

Valensin, George, Artifical Insemination in Women, Trans. Leah Suchodolski, JC, 1960, -------HC, -------PB, NF, 296pp

Webster, Frank, The New Photography: Responsibility in Visual Communication, JC, 1980, Second Impression 1985, 0 7145 3801 9, PB, NF, 262pp

Wallace, Michele, Black Macho and the Myth of the Superwoman, JC, 1979, 0 7145 3778 0, HC, 0 7145 3781 0, PB, NF, 182pp

Wexley, John, The Judgement of Julius and Ethel Rosenberg, B, 1956, ------- , HC, NF, 672pp

Gambit International Theatre Review

Published in Association with Calder and Boyars from Volume 3, Number 11

Volume 3, Number 11, 142pp.
Volume 3, Number 12, 124pp.
Volume 4, Number 13, 128pp
Volume 4, Number 14, **Children's Theatre Issue**, 144pp
Volume 4, Number 15, **The Cat by Otto F. Walter Issue**, 124pp
Volume 4, Number 16, **Breath by Samuel Beckett Issue**, 128pp
Volume 5, Number 17, **Edward Bond Issue**, 128pp
Volume 5, Number 18 and 19, **Heathcote Williams Issue**, 192pp
Volume 5, Number 20, **Le Theatre du Soleil Issue**, 96pp
Volume 6, Number 21, **German Theatre Issue**, 128pp
Volume 6, Number 22, **Ben Johnson Issue**, 112pp
Volume 6, Number 23, **Fringe Theatre Issue**, 128pp
Volume 6, Number 24, 118pp
Volume 7, Number 25, **Playscript Issue**, 118pp
Volume 7, Number 26 and 27, **Television Issue**, 144pp
Volume 7, Number 28, **The National Theatre Issue**, 112pp
Volume 8, Number 29, **Young British Dramatists Issue**, 112pp
Volume 8, Number 30, **French Theatre Issue**, 112pp
Volume 8, Number 31, **Poltical Theater in Britain Issue**, 144pp
Volume 8, Number 32, **Steven Berkoff Issue**, 112pp
Volume 9, Number 33 and 34, **Polish Theatre Issue**, 249pp
Volume 9, Number 35, **Simone Benmussa Issue**, 108pp
Volume 9, Number 36, **Political Theatre in Europe Issue**, 156pp
Volume 10, Number 37, **Tom Stoppard Issue**, 144pp
Volume 10, Number 38, **Theatre and Music Issue**, 168pp
Volume 10, Number 39 and 40, **German Theatre Issue**, 244pp
Volume 11, Number 41, **Howard Barker Special Issue**, 144pp
Volume 11, Number 42 and 43, **Four Belgian Playwrights Issue**, 168pp

Acorn Press for Children

Taylor, J., Boys and Girls Book of Carpentry, AP, 1957, -------HC, F, 96pp
Maurois, Andre, Nico: The Story of a Little French Boy Who Turned Into a Dog, Photographs by Gerald Maurois, AP, 1957, ---------, HC, F Unpaginated
Green David, In the Wood and Other Stories, AP, 1956, -------HC, F, 96pp
Maloney, Terry, Other Worlds in Space, AP, 1957, ------HC, NF, 128pp
Black Margaret, Three Brothers and a Lady, AP, 1957, -------HC, 64pp
Friendenthal, Richard, Goethe Chronicle, AP, (?) -------HC, NF 67pp
Chapman, Jane, The Girl's Book of Sewing, AP, (?) -------, HC, NF, 96pp
Meynell, Laurence, Our Patron Saints, AP, 1957, -------HC, NF, 120pp